Copyright © 2011 by PAGODA Academy, Inc.

All rights reserved. No part of this publication may be reproduced, stored in a retrieval system, or transmitted, in any form, or by any means, electronic, mechanical, photocopying, recording or otherwise, without the prior written permission of the copyright holder and the publisher.

Published by PAGODA Books
PAGODA Books is the professional language publishing company of the PAGODA Education Group.
19F, PAGODA Tower, 419, Gangnam-daero,
Seocho-gu, Seoul, 06614, Rep. of KOREA
www.pagodabook.com

First published 2011
Thirty-first impression 2025
Printed in the Republic of Korea

ISBN 978-89-6281-244-2 (14740)

Publisher | Kyung-Sil Park
Writers | PAGODA Language Education Center

A defective book may be exchanged at the store where you purchased it.

Introduction

i Can Speak 1Blue, the first level of the *i* Can Speak series, is a speaking-focused course book for English learners who are at a very basic level. This book gives learners the opportunity to understand the basics of English structure and become familiar with beginner-level vocabulary and basic expressions. This book also enables students to build up a strong foundation in the fundamentals of conversational English while developing their grammar skills at the same time.

There are 18 lessons in this book and each lesson consists of the following sections:

Warm-Up

This section introduces relevant vocabulary and expressions for each lesson through simple activities. It provides a useful list of new words for beginners. As the lessons proceed, learners will be able to effectively preview the appropriate lexical items for a particular English conversation.

Dialogue

This section covers target sentences in authentic conversations between two people. It also helps listening skills and creates interest in the lesson by using role-play.

Grammar Point

This section provides the English target structures for each lesson. It helps students understand the grammatical forms and functions that are needed to convey meaning accurately.

Practice

This section provides practice drills that make use of the new dialogues using the given words or expressions. This controlled activity allows learners to become familiar with the dialogues using the target structures.

Pair Work

This section offers pair-work activity. It stimulates learners to use the information from the lesson to ask and answer questions with their peers.

Pronunciation

This section provides students with comparison work composed of often-confused sounds. It can be used in various ways; students can either simply listen and repeat the sentences, or they can work in pairs and practice together.

*This course book is used best in collaboration with the on-line program.

Scope and Sequence

Introduction ······· 3
Pronunciation ······· 6
Irregular Verbs ······· 7
Classroom Language ······· 8-9

	Topic	Grammar	Page
Lesson 01 I invited my friends over to my house.	Past Events I	*Simple Past :* Affirmative Statements Negative Statements	10
Lesson 02 What did you do over the weekend?	Past Events II	*Simple Past :* Yes / No Questions Wh-Questions	18
Lesson 03 Do you enjoy summer sports?	Seasonal Activities	*Gerund; enjoy+~ing* Yes / No Questions Wh-Questions	26
Lesson 04 It's a brown leather bag.	Describing Objects	*Adjectives for Describing Objects*	32
Lesson 05 He's tall and muscular.	Physical Appearance	*Adjectives for Describing Appearance*	38
Lesson 06 How often do you do your laundry?	Daily Routines	*Frequency Adverbs Expressions*	44
Lesson 07 It's going to be sunny and warm.	Weather Report	*Future ; be going to :* Affirmative Statements Negative Statements	52
Lesson 08 How are you going to get there?	Transportation and Activities	*Future ; be going to:* Yes / No Questions Wh-Questions	58
Lesson 09 What will you do next year?	Future Plans	*Future ; will :* Affirmative / Negative Statements Yes / No Questions Wh-Questions	64

	Topic	Grammar	Page
Lesson 10 I'd like to book a flight to New York.	Booking a Flight	***Would like to vs. Would like :*** Would like to + verb Would like + noun	70
Lesson 11 May I take your order?	Restaurants	***Modals :*** May, Could, Can (Asking for Permission)	76
Lesson 12 You should see a doctor.	Health Problems	***Modals :*** Should, Have to	82
Lesson 13 The gold ring is prettier than the silver one.	Comparisons of Objects and People	***Comparatives***	88
Lesson 14 He's the funniest guy in the company.	Personalities	***Superlatives***	94
Lesson 15 She has lived in Canada, Spain and Korea.	Past Experiences I	***Present Perfect :*** Past Participles – Regular Verbs Affirmative / Negative Statements	100
Lesson 16 Have you ever been to Hong Kong?	Past Experiences II	***Present Perfect :*** Past Participles – Irregular Verbs Yes / No Questions	108
Lesson 17 The convenience store is next to the coffee shop.	Locations	***Prepositions of Places***	114
Lesson 18 Could you tell me how to get to the library?	Giving Directions	***Imperatives***	120

Pronunciation

/d/, /t/	/d/: **d**og, **d**ay, **d**egree, **d**ress, **d**ream
	/t/: **t**ea, **t**ime, **t**ell, **t**ie, **t**each
/dʒ/, /z/	/dʒ/: **j**acket, **j**eans, **J**anuary, **j**ump
	/z/: **z**ero, **z**ebra, **z**oo, **z**oom
/k/, /g/	/k/: **c**at, **c**andy, **c**lever, **c**ook
	/g/: **g**o, **g**et, **g**lass, **g**ave
/æ/, /e/	/æ/: **a**pple, b**a**d, h**a**nd, h**a**ve, m**a**n
	/e/: m**e**n, **a**ny, h**ea**d, s**ai**d, w**e**nt
/ə/, /ʌ/	/ə/: **a**rrive, doct**o**r, pict**u**re, S**a**turday
	/ʌ/: c**u**t, **u**p, c**o**me, f**u**n, y**ou**ng
/aɪ/, /eɪ/	/aɪ/: l**i**ne, **eye**, f**i**ve, n**i**ce, t**i**me
	/eɪ/: d**ay**, f**a**ce, r**ai**n, w**a**ke, l**a**te
/ɪ/, /iː/	/ɪ/: s**i**t, b**i**g, g**i**ve, l**i**ve, s**i**ng
	/iː/: s**ea**t, b**ea**ch, k**ey**, l**ea**ve, s**ee**

Irregular Verbs

Base Verb	Simple Past	Past Participle
be	was/were	been
build	built	built
buy	bought	bought
come	came	come
do	did	done
drink	drank	drunk
drive	drove	driven
eat	ate	eaten
find	found	found
forget	forgot	forgotten
get	got	gotten
give	gave	given
go	went	gone
have	had	had
hear	heard	heard
keep	kept	kept
lose	lost	lost
make	made	made
meet	met	met
read /ri:d/	read /red/	read /red/
ride	rode	ridden
run	ran	run
say	said	said
see	saw	seen
sing	sang	sung
swim	swam	swum
take	took	taken
tell	told	told
write	wrote	written

Classroom Language

Teacher's Talk

Students' Talk

Lesson 1
I invited my friends over to my house.

Warm-Up *Match the sentences with the pictures.*

— Sentences —

a. She **watched** TV last night.
b. We **walked** home together last night.
c. I **studied** for the exam last weekend.
d. They **worked** late last night.
e. She **opened** the window.
f. We **visited** Paris last summer.
g. We **listened** to her lecture.
h. He **played** basketball yesterday.
i. She **closed** the door.
j. I **invited** some friends over to my house.
k. He **arrived** early to a meeting.
l. I **called** you in the morning.

 **Dialogue** Listen to the dialogue and practice.

Daniel: Jenny, there you are.
I called you yesterday.
Jenny: Oh, I'm sorry.
I was having fun with my friends.
Daniel: I see. What did you do yesterday?
Jenny: *I invited my friends over to my house and we played some games.*
Daniel: Did you play computer games?
Jenny: Oh, no. *We didn't play computer games. We played board games.*
Daniel: Sounds like you had fun yesterday.

Comprehension Check!

Why didn't Jenny answer her phone yesterday?
What did Jenny do yesterday?
Did Jenny and her friends play computer games?

Role-Play

Using the above dialogue, roleplay with your partner using your own personal information.

Grammar Point 1 — *Simple Past Verbs*

Regular Verbs

Rules	Base Verb	Simple Past	Base Verb	Simple Past
verbs → -ed	call	call**ed**	listen	listen**ed**
	visit	visit**ed**	walk	walk**ed**
	watch	watch**ed**	work	work**ed**
-e → -d	arrive	arriv**ed**	invite	invit**ed**
consonant + y → -ied	study	stud**ied**	try	tr**ied**
vowel + y → -ed	play	play**ed**		

Pronunciation Rules

Rules	Examples		Pronunciation
verbs ending in /d/, /t/ sounds	vis**i**ted stud**i**ed	inv**i**ted	/ɪd/
verbs ending in /p/, /f/, /k/, /s/, /sh/, /ch/ sounds	hel**p**ed wal**k**ed	wor**k**ed wat**ch**ed	/t/
verbs ending in other sounds	pla**y**ed liste**n**ed	arri**v**ed ca**ll**ed	/d/

Grammar Point 2   Simple Past: Affirmative / Negative Statements

Affirmative Statements	Negative Statements
I **watched** TV last night.	I **did not watch** TV last night. (= I **didn't watch** TV last night.)
She **listened** to the music yesterday.	She **did not listen** to the music yesterday. (= She **didn't listen** to the music yesterday.)
We **visited** our parents last weekend.	We **did not visit** our parents last weekend. (= We **didn't visit** our parents last weekend.)
They **played** soccer yesterday.	They **did not play** soccer yesterday. (= They **didn't play** soccer yesterday.)

Practice   Practice the dialogue with a partner. See the example below.

watch a romantic comedy / watch a horror movie

Example

A: Melissa didn't watch a romantic comedy yesterday. She watched a horror movie instead.
B: Oh, really? That's surprising. I didn't know that.

1. Cathy

invite her friends for food / invite her friends for drinks

2. David

work late / work out

Lesson 1 • 13

3 Kelly
play the piano / play the violin

4 Crystal
visit New Jersey / visit New York

5 Brian and Wendy
play badminton / play tennis

6 Rick
dance the tango / dance to hip-hop

7 Susie
listen to rock music / listen to classical music

8 Judy and Sally
arrive late for the seminar / arrive early

9 John and Fay
study French / study Chinese

10 Eric
call his boss / call his colleague

Pair Work

Divide the class into pairs. One student will be **Student A**, and the other will be **Student B**. Referring to the sample dialogue below, form questions and answers using the information provided.

☺ : Who worked late last night?
☺ : David and Chris worked late last night.
☺ : Oh, I see. Thanks.

1 Find out the names of the people in the pictures by asking **Student B** questions.

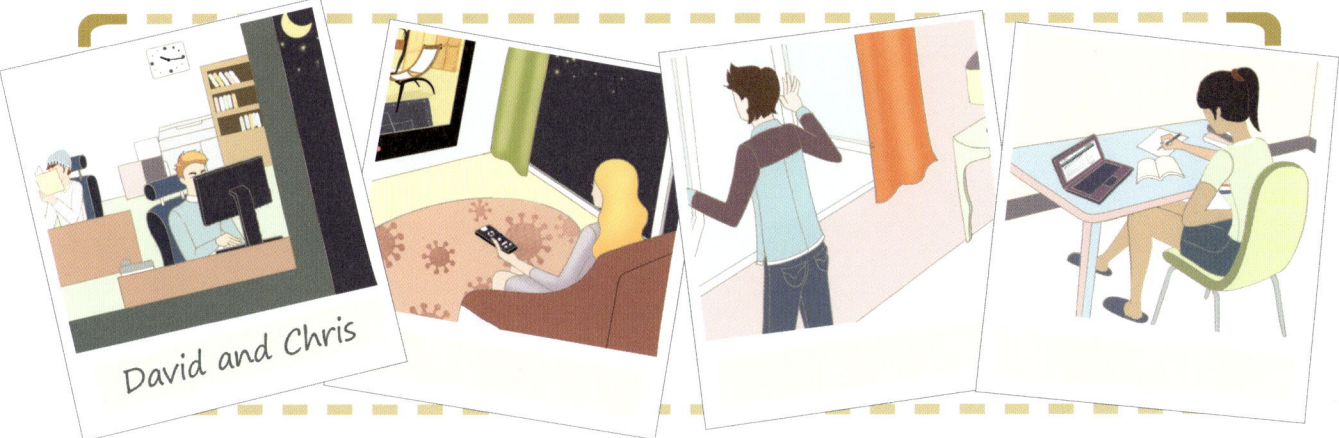

2 Answer **Student B**'s questions by telling him / her the names of the people in the pictures.

Pair Work

STUDENT B

Divide the class into pairs. One student will be **Student A**, and the other will be **Student B**. Referring to the sample dialogue below, form questions and answers using the information provided.

☺ : Who worked late last night?
☺ : David and Chris worked late last night.
☺ : Oh, I see. Thanks.

1 Answer **Student A**'s questions by telling him/her the names of the people in the pictures.

2 Find out the names of the people in the pictures by asking **Student A** questions.

Pronunciation *Listen to the following sentences and repeat after them.*

1. I watch TV every day.
   I watched TV yesterday.

2. He plays baseball every Saturday.
   He played baseball last Saturday.

3. She studies English every Friday.
   She studied English last Friday.

4. They dance the tango every weekend.
   They danced the tango last weekend.

5. We invite my grandparents every Sunday.
   We invited my grandparents last Sunday.

6. I call my sister every day.
   I called my parents yesterday.

Stretch Out!

More Pronunciation

/d/	/t/	/Id/
cried	liked	shouted
tried	washed	landed
loved	helped	wanted
rained	brushed	needed
		ended

Lesson 1 · 17

Lesson 2: What did you do over the weekend?

Warm-Up: Complete the sentences using the appropriate words from the list. Then complete the crossword to find the hidden word.

Word List
bought, made, went, rode, did
ate, came, swam, drank, found
met, read, saw, lost, had

Across →

1. Jane _____ a bike in the park yesterday.
3. They all _____ non-alcohol beverage last night.
6. She _____ home late after work yesterday.
8. They _____ a movie together last weekend.
12~13. Kevin _____ to the beach and _____ in the ocean.
14~15. Nancy _____ her cell phone last week. So, she _____ a new one yesterday.

Down ↓

2. David _____ his assignment over the weekend.
4. I _____ $100 bill on the street yesterday.
5. I _____ lots of homemade cookies for my nephew last Christmas.
7. Tom _____ his professor on the street last Tuesday.
9. She _____ a book until 4 o'clock in the morning.
10~11. We _____ Italian food for dinner. I _____ seafood pasta.

Crossword

→ The hidden word is _____

Dialogue
Listen to the dialogue and practice.

Robert: Susan, how was your weekend?
Susan: It was fun.
Robert: Really? *What did you do over the weekend?*
Susan: *I went to the east coast with my friends. We swam in the ocean and got a suntan.* How was yours? You look a little bit tired today.
Robert: That's right. I'm tired. *I met my friends and had some beer.*

Comprehension Check!
Did Susan have a good weekend?
Where did Susan go over the weekend?
Who did Susan go with?
What did Robert do over the weekend?

Role-Play
Using the above dialogue, roleplay with your partner using your own personal information.

Grammar Point 1 *Simple Past Verbs*

Irregular Verbs

Base Verb	Simple Past	Base Verb	Simple Past
buy	**bought**	come	**came**
do	**did**	drink	**drank**
eat	**ate**	have	**had**
go	**went**	get	**got**
find	**found**	lose	**lost**
make	**made**	meet	**met**
read /ri:d/	**read** /red/	ride	**rode**
swim	**swam**	see	**saw**

Grammar Point 2 *Simple Past: Yes/No Questions*

Yes/No Questions	Short Answers	
Did you **buy** something yesterday?	Yes, I **did**.	No, I **didn't**. (**= did not**)
Did he **swim** last Saturday?	Yes, he **did**.	No, he **didn't**.
Did they **go** to the beach?	Yes, they **did**.	No, they **didn't**.

Grammar Point 3 *Simple Past: Wh-questions*

Wh-Questions	Answers
What did you **do** last Thursday?	I **saw** a movie last Thursday.
What did she **do** yesterday?	She **went** to the zoo yesterday.
What did they **do** last weekend?	They **made** pizza last weekend.

Practice
Practice the dialogue with a partner. See the example below.

see a movie | clean her house

Example

A: What did **Jane** do last weekend?
B: **She saw a movie** on Saturday.
A: Did **she see a movie** on Sunday too?
B: No, **she** didn't. **She cleaned her house** on Sunday.

swim in the ocean | eat some seafood

go to an amusement park | watch TV at home

Chris and Liz

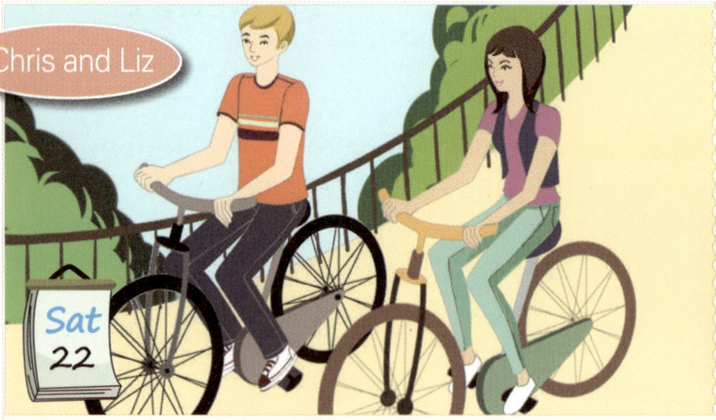

ride a bike

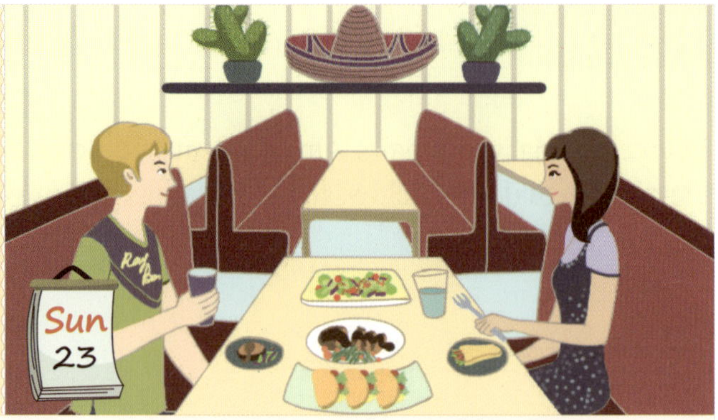

have Mexican food

Adam

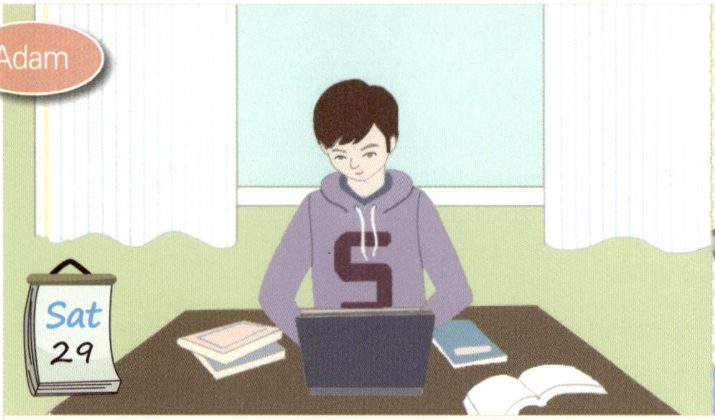

do his assignment

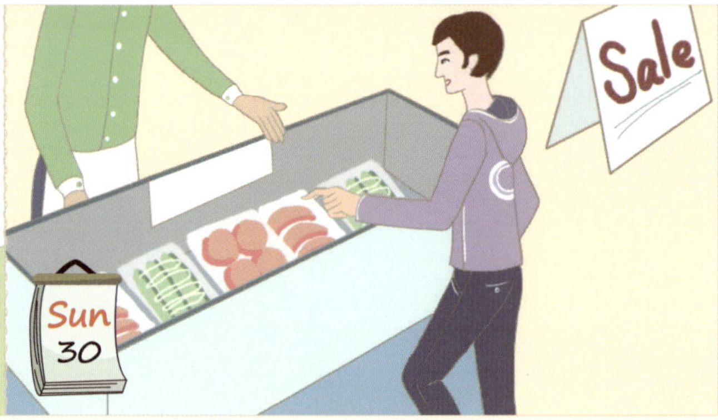

buy some food

Clare

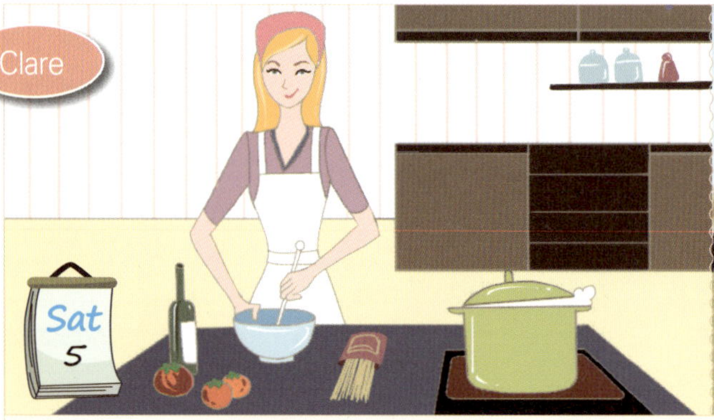

make spaghetti

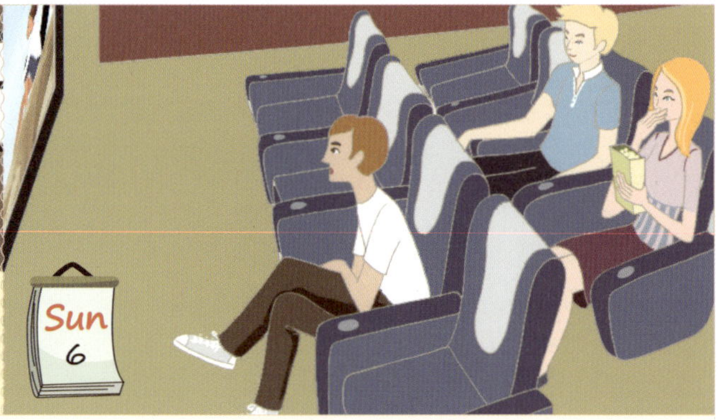

see a movie

Ellison

go shopping

read books

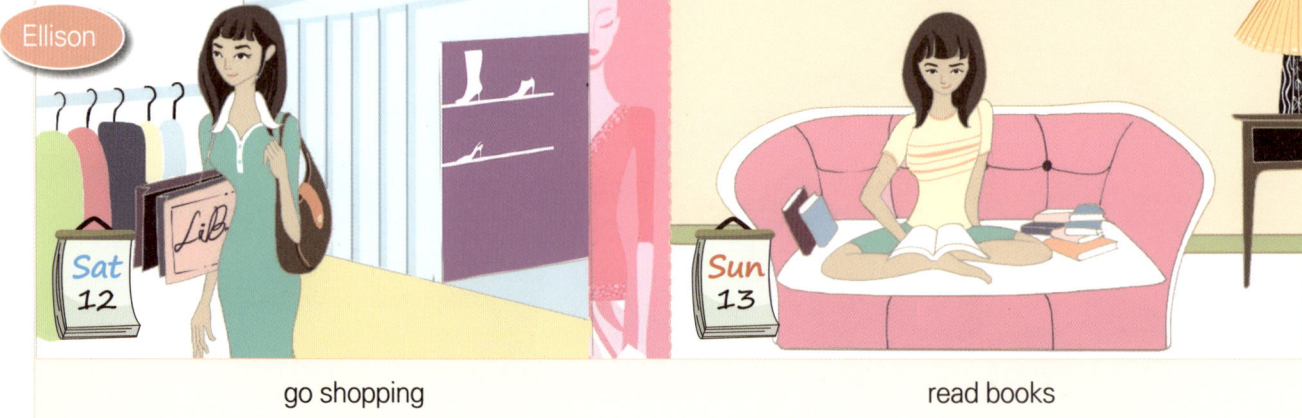

Pair Work

STUDENT A

Divide the class into pairs. One student will be **Student A**, and the other will be **Student B**. Referring to the sample dialogue below, form questions and answers using the information provided.

☺ : Hey, **Kevin**. How was your weekend?

☺ : Oh, I had a great weekend.
☺ : Wow! What did you do?
☺ : I went to an amusement park and rode a rollercoaster.
☺ : Did you enjoy it?
☺ : Yes, I enjoyed it a lot.

☹ : Oh, I had a horrible weekend.
☺ : Really? What did you do?
☹ : I went to an amusement park and lost a $100 bill.
☺ : Oh, no! I'm sorry.
☹ : It's OK.

1 Ask **Student B** questions about the information in the chart. Check (✓) whether each person listed below had a good weekend or not. Then write what he / she did on the weekend.

Your Partner	☺	☹	What did your partner do on the weekend?
Derrick	☐	☐	
Jasmine	☐	☐	
Andrew	☐	☐	
Vivian	☐	☐	

2 Imagine you are the person listed below. Answer **Student B**'s questions based on the information below. Change the verbs into correct forms when answering the questions.

You	☺	☹	What did you do on the weekend?	
Gina	✓	☐	**go** to a park	**ride** a bicycle
Sean	☐	✓	**drink** alcohol	**get** sick
Katrina	☐	✓	**work** in the office	**come** home late
Taylor	✓	☐	**have** a date with my girlfriend	**see** a movie

Lesson 2 · 23

Pair Work

STUDENT B

Divide the class into pairs. One student will be **Student A**, and the other will be **Student B**. Referring to the sample dialogue below, form questions and answers using the information provided.

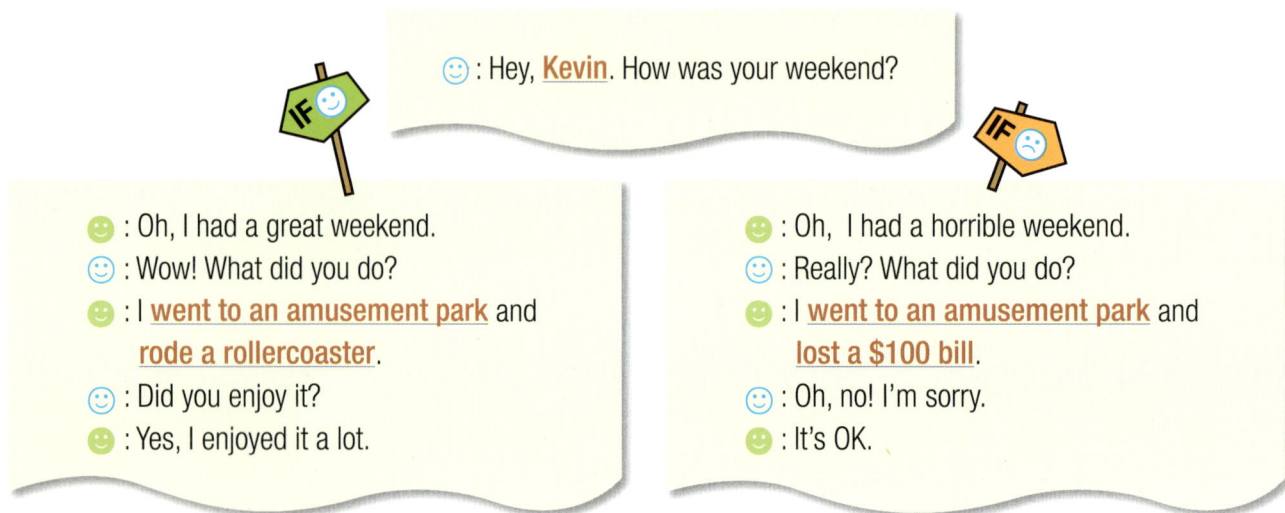

☺ : Hey, Kevin. How was your weekend?

☺ : Oh, I had a great weekend.
☺ : Wow! What did you do?
☺ : I went to an amusement park and rode a rollercoaster.
☺ : Did you enjoy it?
☺ : Yes, I enjoyed it a lot.

☺ : Oh, I had a horrible weekend.
☺ : Really? What did you do?
☺ : I went to an amusement park and lost a $100 bill.
☺ : Oh, no! I'm sorry.
☺ : It's OK.

1 Imagine you are the person listed below. Answer **Student A**'s questions based on the information below. Change the verbs into correct forms when answering the questions.

You	☺	☹	What did you do on the weekend?	
Derrick		✓	**lose** my wallet	**walk** home
Jasmine	✓		**meet** my friends	**eat** a lot of delicious food
Andrew	✓		**go** on a picnic	**play** baseball
Vivian		✓	**swim** in the ocean	**get** a cold

2 Ask **Student A** questions about the information in the chart. Check (✓) whether each person listed below had a good weekend or not. Then write what he / she did on the weekend.

Your Partner	☺	☹	What did your partner do on the weekend?
Gina	☐	☐	
Sean	☐	☐	
Katrina	☐	☐	
Taylor	☐	☐	

 **Pronunciation** Listen to the following sentences and repeat after them.

1. What did he do on the weekend?
   What did she do on the weekend?

2. Did he go shopping last Saturday?
   Did she go shopping last Saturday?

3. I eat some vegetables every day.
   I ate some vegetables yesterday.

4. He buys milk every morning.
   He bought milk yesterday.

5. She reads books every night.
   She read books last night.

Stretch Out!

More Irregular Verbs

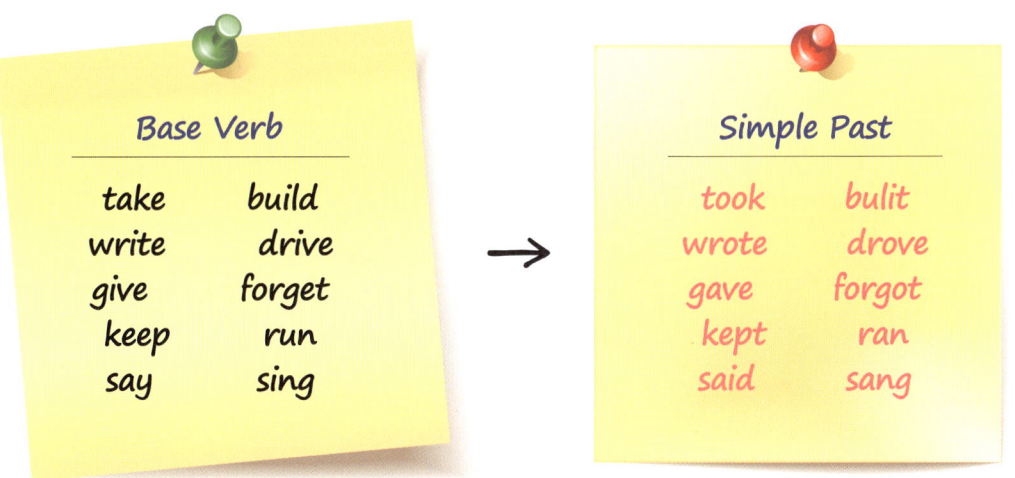

Base Verb		Simple Past	
take	build	took	bulit
write	drive	wrote	drove
give	forget	gave	forgot
keep	run	kept	ran
say	sing	said	sang

Lesson 3: Do you enjoy summer sports?

Warm-Up *Put the appropriate activities from the list in the box for each season.*

– Expressions –

snowboarding	swimming	skating	camping
taking pictures	rafting	going on picnics	(ice) fishing
bungee jumping	waterskiing	hiking	planting flowers
scuba diving	sledding	sightseeing	having a snowball fight
skiing	riding a bike	jogging	playing beach volleyball

- Spring
- Summer
- Autumn / Fall
- Winter
- All seasons

Dialogue Listen to the dialogue and practice.

Julia: Oh, this heat is killing me! I hate summer.
Ian: Really? I like summer.
Julia: **Do you enjoy summer sports?**
Ian: **Yes, I do. I enjoy scuba diving.**
What is your favorite season then?
Julia: Spring.
Ian: Hmm… why is that?
Julia: It's because I like nice and warm weather and **I enjoy going on picnics.**

Comprehension Check!
What sports does Ian enjoy doing?
What does Julia enjoy doing in spring?

Role-Play
Using the above dialogue, roleplay with your partner using your own personal information.

Grammar Point Gerund (enjoy + –ing)

Yes / No Questions	Answers
Do you **enjoy snowboarding** in winter?	Yes, I do. No, I don't. I **enjoy skiing** in winter.
Does he **enjoy rafting** in summer?	Yes, he does. No, he doesn't. He **enjoys swimming** in summer.

Wh-Questions	Answers
What do you **enjoy doing** in fall?	I **enjoy going camping** in fall.
What does she **enjoy doing** in spring?	She **enjoys sightseeing** in spring.

Lesson 3 · 27

Practice
Practice the dialogue with a partner. See the example below.

winter / ski

Example

A: What is your favorite season?
B: It's <u>winter</u>.
A: I see. What do you enjoy doing in <u>winter</u>?
B: I enjoy <u>skiing</u>. What about you?
    Which season do you like most?
A: I like <u>spring</u>. That's because I enjoy <u>going on picnics</u>.

spring / go on picnics

1.
winter / skate

summer / scuba dive

2.
autumn / camp

summer / tan

3.
summer / raft

winter / snowboard

4.
winter / have a snowball fight

summer / swim in the ocean

5.
autumn / hike

winter / sled

6.
spring / take pictures of flowers

summer / play beach volleyball

Pair Work

STUDENT A

Divide the class into pairs. One student will be **Student A**, and the other will be **Student B**. Referring to the sample dialogue below, form questions and answers using the information provided.

😊 : What is **Scott**'s favorite season?
🙂 : **Summer**. **He** enjoys **swimming**.
😊 : What else **does he** enjoy doing in **summer**?
🙂 : **He** enjoys **rafting**.
😊 : I see. **Summer** is one of my favorite seasons as well.

1 Ask **Student B** questions about the information in the chart. Check (✓) which season the people and **Student B** like and write their reasons.

	Favorite Season				Reasons
Anna	☐	☐	☐	☐	• •
Ron	☐	☐	☐	☐	• •
Student B (Your Partner)	☐	☐	☐	☐	• •

2 Check (✓) which season you like the best and write reasons. Then answer **Student B**'s questions based on the information below.

	Favorite Season				Reasons
Wendy	✓	☐	☐	☐	• take pictures of flowers • go on picnics
David	☐	✓	☐	☐	• play on the beach • scuba dive
Student A (You)	☐	☐	☐	☐	• •

Lesson 3 · 29

Pair Work

STUDENT B

Divide the class into pairs. One student will be **Student A**, and the other will be **Student B**. Referring to the sample dialogue below, form questions and answers using the information provided.

☺ : What is Scott's favorite season?
☺ : Summer. He enjoys swimming.
☺ : What else does he enjoy doing in summer?
☺ : He enjoys rafting.
☺ : I see. Summer is one of my favorite seasons as well.

1 Check (✓) which season you like the best and write reasons. Then answer **Student A**'s questions based on the information below.

	Favorite Season				Reasons
Anna	☐	☐	✓	☐	• camp • hike
Ron	☐	☐	☐	✓	• have a snowball fight • skate
Student B (You)	☐	☐	☐	☐	• •

2 Ask **Student A** questions about the information in the chart. Check (✓) which season the people and **Student B** like and write their reasons.

	Favorite Season				Reasons
Wendy	☐	☐	☐	☐	• •
David	☐	☐	☐	☐	• •
Student A (Your Partner)	☐	☐	☐	☐	• •

Pronunciation
Listen to the following sentences and repeat after them.

1
She enjoys rafting.
They enjoy rafting.

2
I enjoy skating in winter.
He enjoys skiing in winter.

3
What does he enjoy doing?
What does she enjoy doing?

4
What do you enjoy doing in spring?
What do they enjoy doing in fall?

5
Does he enjoy bungee jumping?
Does she enjoy bungee jumping?

6
Do you enjoy playing beach volleyball in summer?
Do you enjoy playing golf in summer?

Stretch Out!
More Seasonal Sports

(wind) surfing	canoeing
waterskiing	snorkeling
paragliding	rock climbing
car racing	bobsleighing
golfing	horse riding

Lesson 4
It's a brown leather bag.

Warm-Up Choose the related words from the list to describe each item.

Colors		Patterns	Materials
red	brown	checkered	leather
orange	gray	plaid	silk
yellow	black	flowered	wool
green	white	plain	paper
blue	pink	polka-dot	cotton
navy	purple	striped	

It's a _____, _____, scarf.

It's a _____, _____, tie.

It's a _____, _____, skirt.

It's a _____, _____, sweater.

It's a _____, _____, shoulder bag.

It's a _____, _____, shirt.

Dialogue *Listen to the dialogue and practice.*

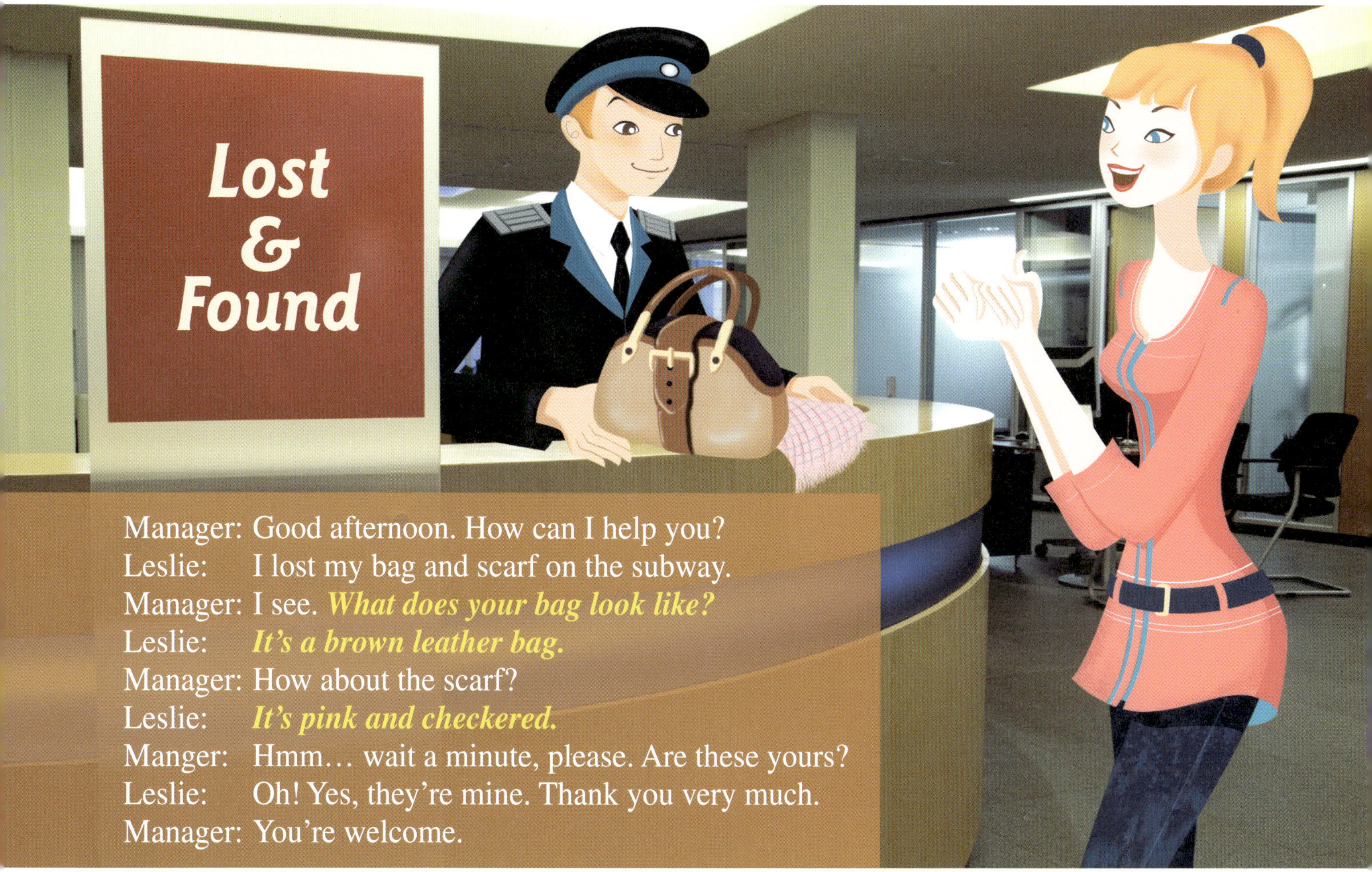

Manager: Good afternoon. How can I help you?
Leslie: I lost my bag and scarf on the subway.
Manager: I see. **What does your bag look like?**
Leslie: **It's a brown leather bag.**
Manager: How about the scarf?
Leslie: **It's pink and checkered.**
Manger: Hmm… wait a minute, please. Are these yours?
Leslie: Oh! Yes, they're mine. Thank you very much.
Manager: You're welcome.

Comprehension Check!

What does Leslie's bag look like?　|　What does her scarf look like?

Role-Play

Using the above dialogue, roleplay with your partner using your own personal information.

Grammar Point 1 *Describing Objects*

Grammar Point 2 *Questions about Objects*

Questions	Answers
What does your shirt look like?	It's **green and striped**. It's **a green striped shirt**.
What is it made of?	It's made of **cotton**.
What do your socks look like?	They're **plain and brown**. They're **plain brown socks**.
What are they made of?	They're made of **wool**.

Practice *Practice the dialogue with a partner. See the example below.*

hat / gray / wool

Example

A: Excuse me.
B: Yes, how may I help you?
A: Hmm… I'm looking for <u>a hat</u>.
B: How about <u>this gray hat</u>?
A: Oh, I like <u>it</u>. What <u>is it</u> made of?
B: <u>It's</u> made of <u>wool</u>.

❶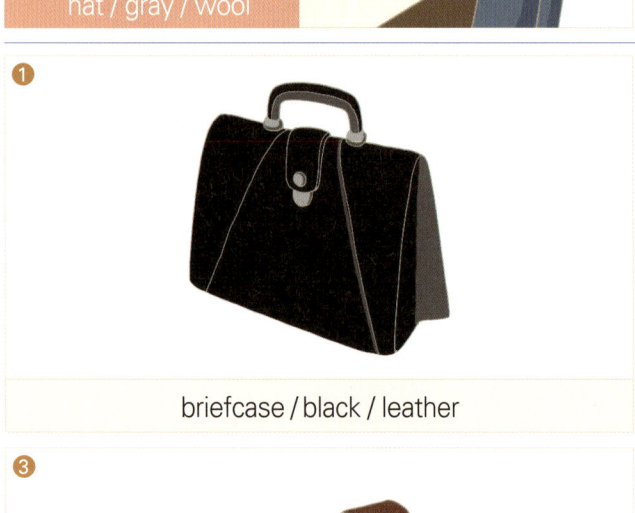

briefcase / black / leather

❷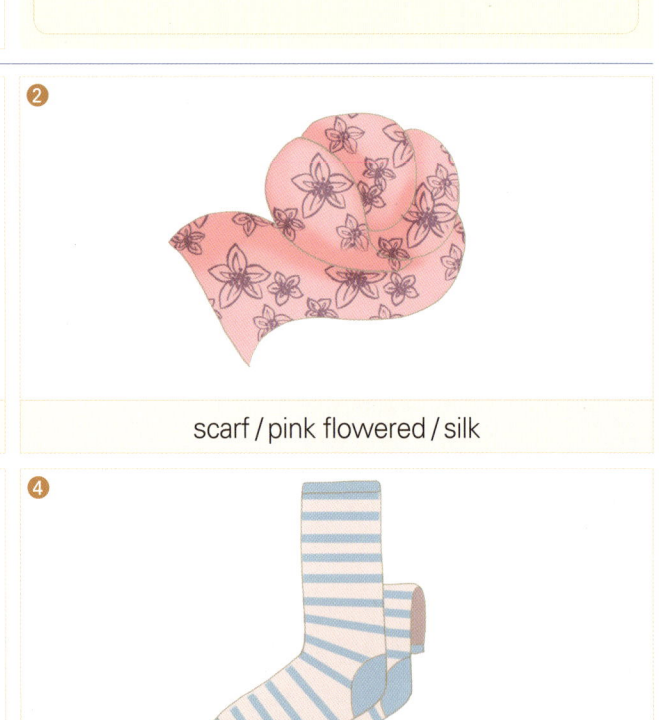

scarf / pink flowered / silk

❸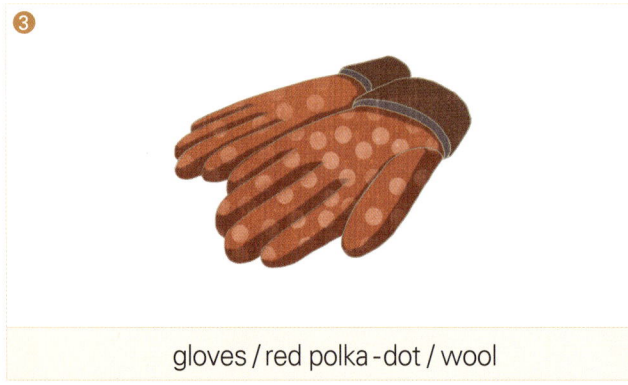

gloves / red polka-dot / wool

❹

socks / pink and blue striped / cotton

Pair Work

STUDENT A

Divide the class into pairs. One student will be **Student A**, and the other will be **Student B**. Referring to the sample dialogue below, form questions and answers using the information provided.

☺ : Thank you for inviting me to your housewarming party.
☺ : You're very welcome. Are you enjoying the party?
☺ : Yes, I am. Is <u>Brian</u> here?
☺ : Yes, <u>he</u> is.
☺ : I can't find <u>him</u>. Where is <u>he</u>?
☺ : <u>He</u>'s over there. <u>He</u>'s wearing <u>a white shirt and blue striped pants</u>.
☺ : Oh, there <u>he</u> is. Thanks.

Ask each other questions to find out where the people are and write their names in the picture.

~~Brian~~
Jennifer
Danny
Cindy
Kevin

Brian
Sarah
Melissa
Fred
Tim

Lesson 4 • 35

Pair Work

 **STUDENT B**

Divide the class into pairs. One student will be **Student A**, and the other will be **Student B**. Referring to the sample dialogue below, form questions and answers using the information provided.

😊 : Thank you for inviting me to your housewarming party.
🙂 : You're very welcome. Are you enjoying the party?
😊 : Yes, I am. Is Brian here?
🙂 : Yes, he is.
😊 : I can't find him. Where is he?
🙂 : He's over there. He's wearing a white shirt and blue striped pants.
😊 : Oh, there he is. Thanks.

Ask each other questions to find out where the people are and write their names in the picture.

~~Brian~~
Sarah
Fred
Melissa
Tim

Labels in picture: Brian, Kevin, Jennifer, Danny, Cindy

Pronunciation Listen to the following sentences and repeat after them.

1 What's *her* bag like?
What's *his* bag like?

2 What's *he* wearing?
What's *she* wearing?

3 It's a green *plain* shirt.
It's a green *plaid* shirt.

4 She's wearing a *brown* leather watch.
He's wearing a *black* leather watch.

5 What *is it* made of?
What *are they* made of?

Stretch Out!

More Words to Describe Objects

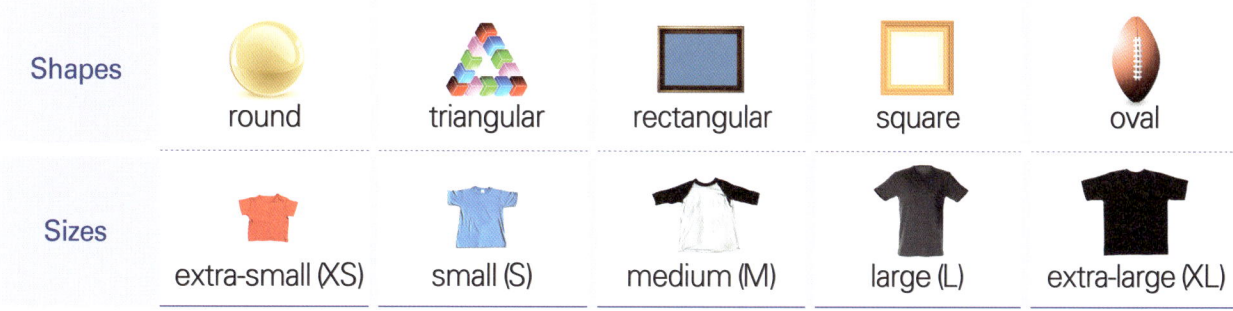

| Shapes | round | triangular | rectangular | square | oval |

| Sizes | extra-small (XS) | small (S) | medium (M) | large (L) | extra-large (XL) |

What *shape* is it? → It's *round*.
What *size* is this shirt? → It's *medium size*.

Lesson 4 · 37

Lesson 5
He's tall and muscular.

Warm-Up Fill in the chart to describe each person, using words from the list.

Height	Weight	Hair
short	skinny slim (thin)	bald short long
average height	average weight	shoulder-length
tall	chubby muscular	straight wavy curly
	overweight	blond brown black red

	Height	Weight	Hair
Kate			
Eric			
Christina			
Ronald			

Dialogue

Listen to the dialogue and practice.

Kevin: Hey, I'm glad you came. Who are you with?
Nancy: I'm with my boyfriend. He's over there.
Kevin: Oh, really? Which one is your boyfriend? *What does he look like?*
Nancy: *He's tall and muscular. And he has short brown hair.*
Kevin: Hmm… is he wearing a white shirt and blue jeans?
Nancy: Yes, he is. That's my boyfriend.
Kevin: I see. Enjoy the party.

Comprehension Check!

Who is Nancy with at the party?
What does Nancy's boyfriend look like? | What is he wearing?

Role-Play

Using the above dialogue, roleplay with your partner using your own personal information.

Grammar Point 1 — Describing Physical Appearance

Height	short		average height			tall
Weight	skinny	slim (thin)	average weight	muscular	chubby	overweight

Hair						
	Length	bald	short	shoulder-length	long	
	Style	straight	wavy	curly		
	Color	blond	brown	black	red	

Grammar Point 2 Questions to Describe Physical Appearence

Questions	Answers
What does she look like?	She's average height and chubby. She has curly brown hair.
What does he look like?	He's tall and thin. He has black hair.

Practice Practice the dialogue with a partner. See the example below.

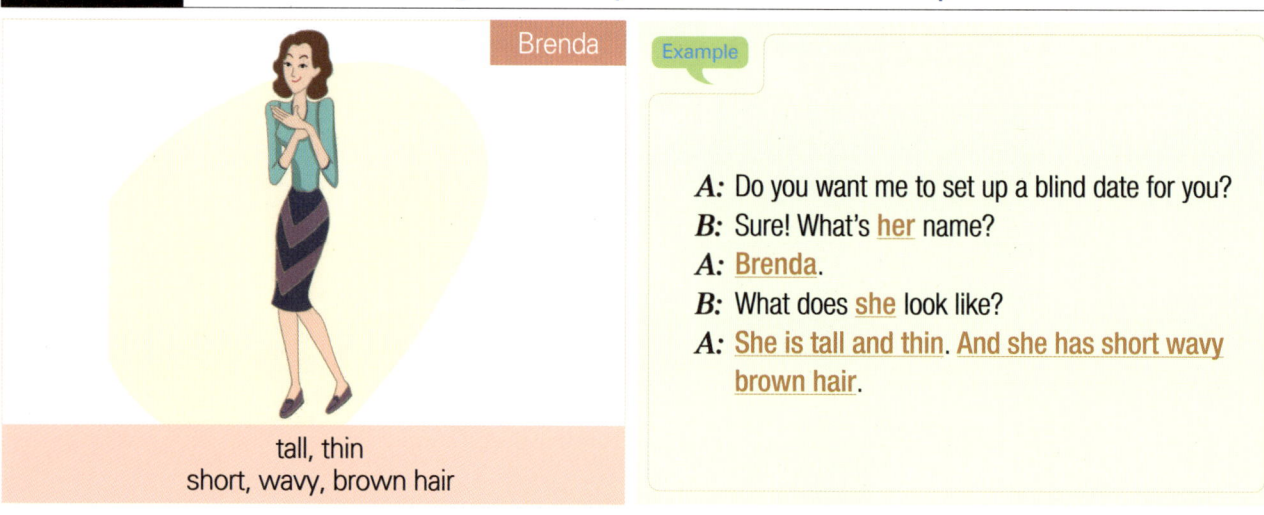

Brenda
tall, thin
short, wavy, brown hair

Example

A: Do you want me to set up a blind date for you?
B: Sure! What's her name?
A: Brenda.
B: What does she look like?
A: She is tall and thin. And she has short wavy brown hair.

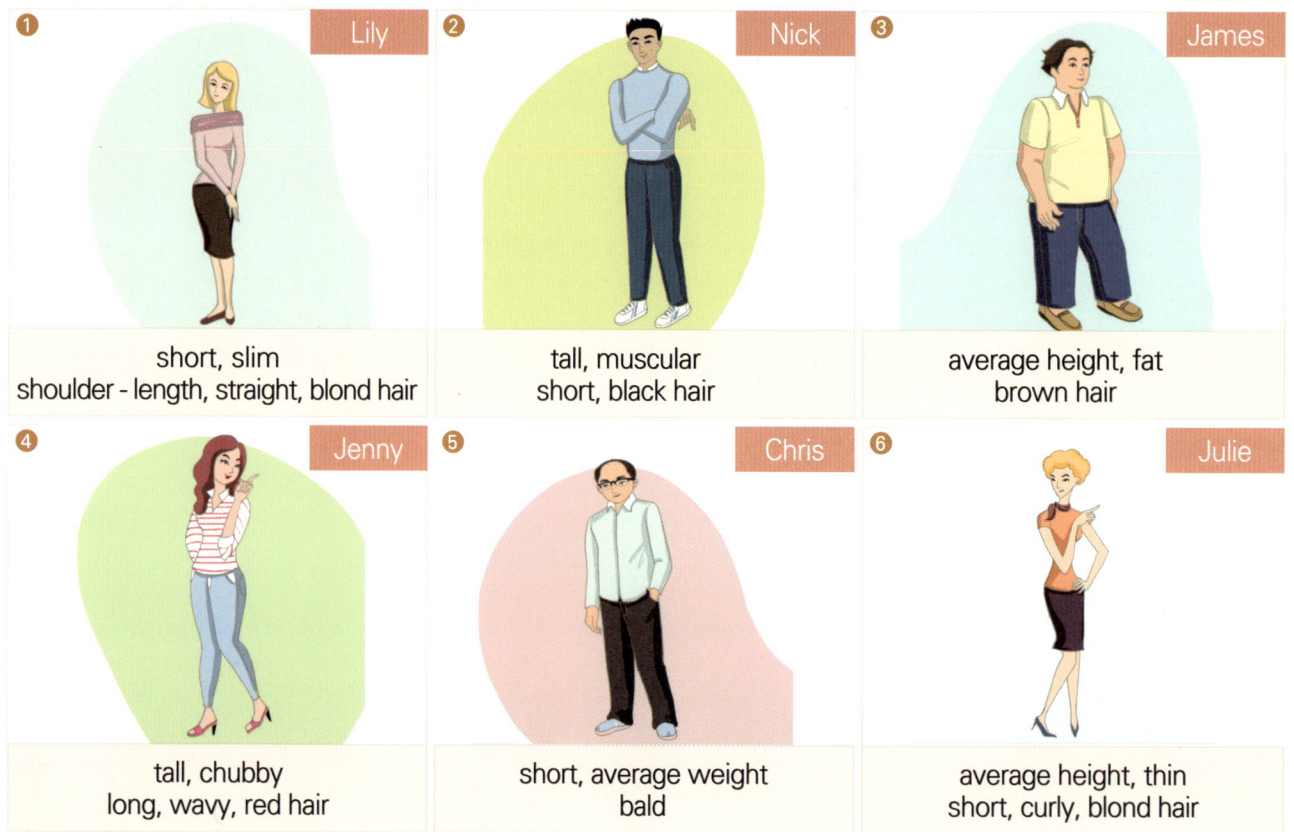

1. Lily — short, slim / shoulder-length, straight, blond hair
2. Nick — tall, muscular / short, black hair
3. James — average height, fat / brown hair
4. Jenny — tall, chubby / long, wavy, red hair
5. Chris — short, average weight / bald
6. Julie — average height, thin / short, curly, blond hair

Pair Work

STUDENT A

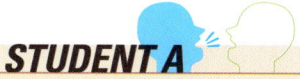

Divide the class into pairs. One student will be ***Student A***, and the other will be ***Student B***. Referring to the sample dialogue below, form questions and answers using the information provided.

- : Could you tell me about Paul?
- : Sure. What do you want to know about him?
- : How old is he?
- : He's 32.
- : What does he look like?
- : He's average height and slim, and he has short black hair.
- : What does he enjoy doing in his free time?
- : He enjoys swimming.
- : Thanks for the information.
- : You're welcome.

1 Ask each other questions to fill in the blank profiles.

Amy age:
- Occupation:
- Height:
- Weight:
- Hair:
- Free time activity:

Daniel age: 35
- Occupation: office worker
- Height: tall
- Weight: average weight
- Hair: short, blond
- Free time activity: scuba diving

Kelly age:
- Occupation:
- Height:
- Weight:
- Hair:
- Free time activity:

Philip age: 32
- Occupation: accountant
- Height: average height
- Weight: fat
- Hair: bald
- Free time activity: taking photos

Carol age:
- Occupation:
- Height:
- Weight:
- Hair:
- Free time activity:

Jason age: 29
- Occupation: fire fighter
- Height: tall
- Weight: muscular
- Hair: brown
- Free time activity: bowling

2 Read the profiles above. Who would you most want to have a blind date with? ________

Pair Work

 **STUDENT B**

Divide the class into pairs. One student will be **Student A**, and the other will be **Student B**. Referring to the sample dialogue below, form questions and answers using the information provided.

> ☺ : Could you tell me about <u>Paul</u>?
> ☺ : Sure. What do you want to know about <u>him</u>?
> ☺ : How old is <u>he</u>?
> ☺ : <u>He's 32</u>.
> ☺ : What does <u>he</u> look like?
> ☺ : <u>He's average height and slim, and he has short black hair</u>.
> ☺ : What does <u>he</u> enjoy doing in <u>his</u> free time?
> ☺ : <u>He enjoys swimming</u>.
> ☺ : Thanks for the information.
> ☺ : You're welcome.

1 Ask each other questions to fill in the blank profiles.

Amy — age: 24
Occupation: nurse
Height: short
Weight: chubby
Hair: short, curly, red
Free time activity: playing the flute

Daniel — age:
Occupation:
Height:
Weight:
Hair:
Free time activity:

Kelly — age: 27
Occupation: researcher
Height: average height
Weight: slim
Hair: long, wavy, black
Free time activity: rafting

Philip — age:
Occupation:
Height:
Weight:
Hair:
Free time activity:

Carol — age: 34
Occupation: teacher
Height: short
Weight: thin
Hair: shoulder-length straight blond
Free time activity: jogging

Jason — age:
Occupation:
Height:
Weight:
Hair:
Free time activity:

2 Read the profiles above. Who would you most want to have a blind date with? ☐

Pronunciation Listen to the following sentences and repeat after them.

1. What does he look like?
   What does she look like?

2. He's tall and average weight.
   She's chubby and average height.

3. Is she short and slim?
   Is he tall and thin?

4. Does he have short brown hair?
   Does she have shoulder-length black hair?

5. I have long black hair.
   She has long blond hair.

6. She has wavy black hair.
   She has curly brown hair.

Stretch Out!

More Words to Describe Appearance

 He has a beard.

 He has a mustache.

 He has sideburns.

 She wears glasses.

 She has freckles.

Lesson 6: How often do you do your laundry?

Warm-Up Referring to Sam's monthly schedule, match the correct expressions from the list below to complete the sentences.

– Expressions –

| drive | work out | go out for a drink | go hiking |
| go to a lunch appointment | | get a haircut | check his e-mail |

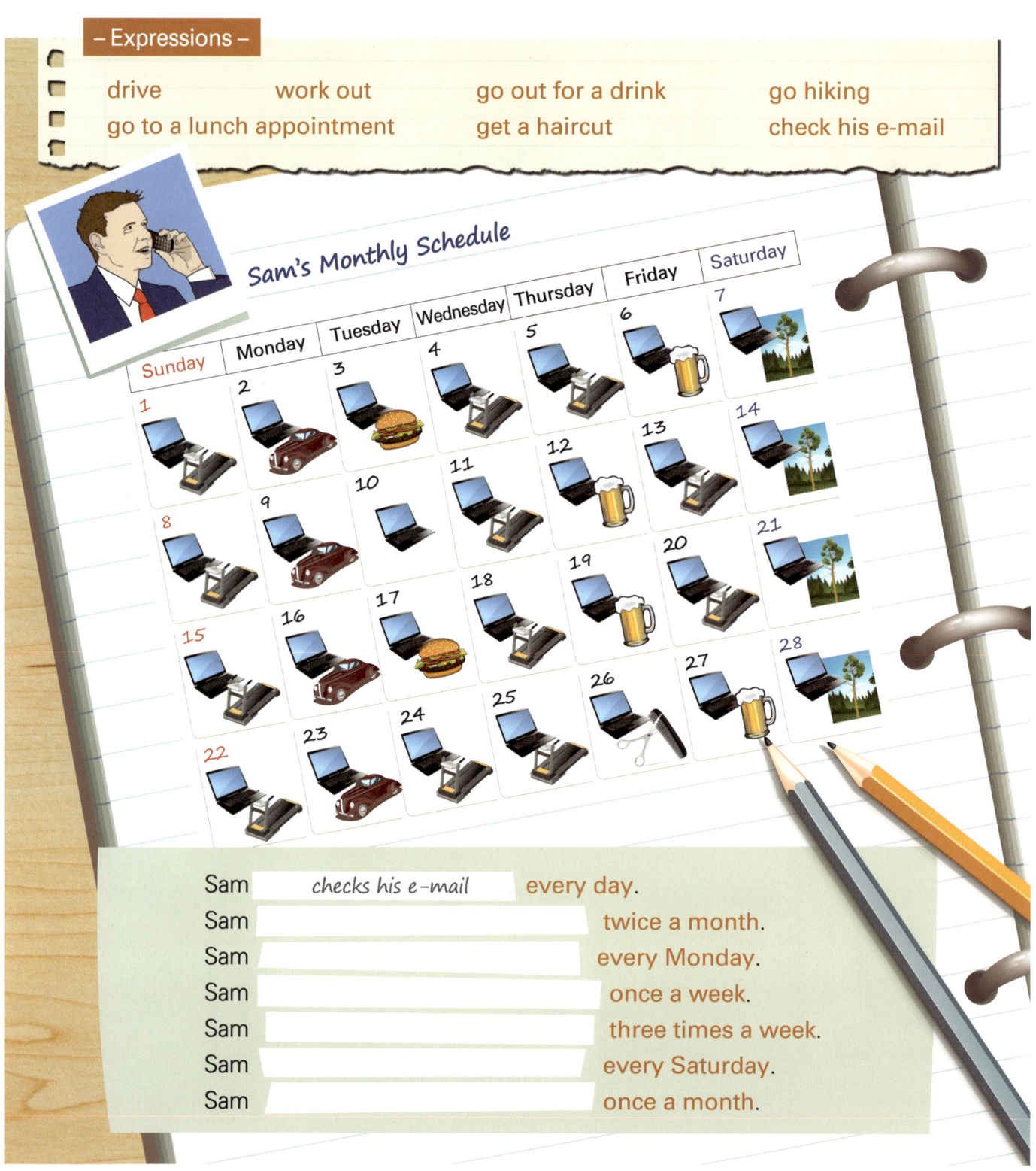

Sam _checks his e-mail_ every day.
Sam ____ twice a month.
Sam ____ every Monday.
Sam ____ once a week.
Sam ____ three times a week.
Sam ____ every Saturday.
Sam ____ once a month.

◆ **Referring to Nancy's monthly schedule, match the correct expressions from the list below to complete the sentences.**

– Expressions –

take the bus to school   study in the library   do the laundry
play computer games   go shopping
clean the house   practice the piano

Nancy always   practices the piano   .
Nancy usually _____.
Nancy rarely _____.
Nancy sometimes _____.
Nancy never _____.
Nancy _____ every Friday.
Nancy _____ once a month.

Lesson 6 · 45

Dialogue
Listen to the dialogue and practice.

Julie: Peter, you look so tired today. What did you do over the weekend?
Peter: Hmm… I did the laundry and cleaned up the house over the weekend.
Julie: Wow! *Do you usually clean up the house on weekends?*
Peter: *No, I rarely do it.*
Julie: I see. Then *how often do you do the laundry?*
Peter: *Probably once a month.* I'm so exhausted now. I don't like doing household chores on the weekend.

Comprehension Check!
Does Peter look energetic today?
What did Peter do over the weekend?
Does Peter usually clean up the house?
How often does Peter do the laundry?

Role-Play
Using the above dialogue, roleplay with your partner using your own personal information.

Grammar Point 1 — Frequency Adverbs & Expressions

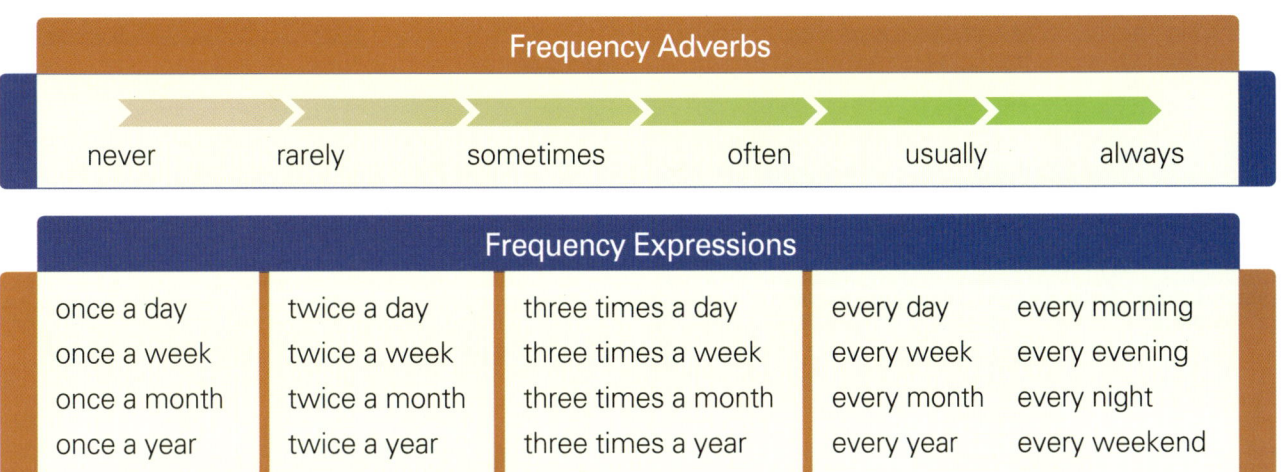

Frequency Adverbs					
never	rarely	sometimes	often	usually	always

Frequency Expressions				
once a day	twice a day	three times a day	every day	every morning
once a week	twice a week	three times a week	every week	every evening
once a month	twice a month	three times a month	every month	every night
once a year	twice a year	three times a year	every year	every weekend

Grammar Point 2 — Placement of Frequency Words

Placement of Frequency Adverbs

He **always** drives to work.
    usually
    often
    sometimes
    rarely
    never

Placement of Frequency Expressions

He drives to work **once a week**.
    twice a week.
    three times a week.
    every day.
    every Monday.

Grammar Point 3 — Questions

Questions	Answers
Do you **usually / often / always** drive to work?	Yes, I **usually / often / always** drive to work. No, I **never / rarely / sometimes** drive to work.
Does she **usually / often / always** go hiking?	Yes, she **usually / often / always** goes hiking. No, she doesn't **usually / often / always** go hiking.
How often do you get a haircut?	I get a haircut **every month**.
How often does he do the laundry?	He does the laundry **twice a week**.

Practice

Practice the dialogue with a partner. See the example below.

Fred
the bus to work
once a month / take the subway to work

Example

A: **Does Fred** usually **take the bus to work**?
B: No, **he** rarely **does** that.
A: I see… Then how often **does he take the bus to work**?
B: Hmm… Maybe **once a month**. He usually **takes the subway to work**.

❶

Kevin
eat out
twice a month / eat at home

❷

you
study in the library
once a month / study at home

❸

Rachel and Tom
go out for a drink
five times a year / go to the movies

❹

Crystal
practice the piano
twice a month / practice the guitar

❺

Eric and Janice
go hiking
once a month / go swimming

❻

you
drive to work
twice a month / take the bus

i Can Speak 1 Blue

Pair Work

Divide the class into pairs. One student will be **Student A**, and the other will be **Student B**. Referring to the sample dialogue below, form questions and answers using the information provided.

Ask your partner questions to complete the survey below.

Partner's name: _____

Do you...?		Yes	No	If yes, how often ....?
1. go shopping		☐	☐	
2. do the laundry		☐	☐	
3. clean the house		☐	☐	
4. play computer games		☐	☐	
5. practice the piano		☐	☐	
6. listen to classical music		☐	☐	
7. take the bus to school / work		☐	☐	
8. drive to school / work		☐	☐	
9. go out for a drink		☐	☐	
10. work out		☐	☐	

Lesson 6 • 49

Pair Work

 **STUDENT B**

Divide the class into pairs. One student will be **Student A**, and the other will be **Student B**. Referring to the sample dialogue below, form questions and answers using the information provided.

- 😊 : Can I ask you something?
- 🙂 : Sure, go ahead.
- 😊 : Do you go hiking?
- 🙂 : Yes, I do.
- 😊 : How often do you go hiking?
- 🙂 : I go hiking every weekend.
- 😊 : I see. Then do you …?

  continue

- 😊 : Can I ask you something?
- 🙂 : Sure, go ahead.
- 😊 : Do you go hiking?
- 🙂 : No, I don't. I never go hiking.
- 😊 : I see. Then do you …?

  continue

Ask your partner questions to complete the survey below.

Partner's name: _____

Do you...?		Yes	No	If yes, how often ....?
1. go hiking		☐	☐	
2. do the dishes		☐	☐	
3. wash your car		☐	☐	
4. play basketball		☐	☐	
5. practice the guitar		☐	☐	
6. listen to rock music		☐	☐	
7. eat out		☐	☐	
8. go to the movies		☐	☐	
9. take the subway to school / work		☐	☐	
10. get a medical check-up		☐	☐	

Pronunciation Listen to the following sentences and repeat after them.

1 Do you usually go out for a drink?
Do you always go out for a drink?

2 He rarely gets a medical check-up.
He never gets a medical check-up.

3 She drives to work once a week.
He drives to work twice a week.

4 I eat out every weekend.
She eats out every other Wednesday.

5 How often does he work out?
How often does she work out?

6 They go hiking once a week.
They go hiking once a month.

Stretch Out!

More Useful Expressions

▸ Do you often ...?
   travel abroad
   go to parties
   go for a drive
   invite your friends over to your house
   visit your parents
   go to a sauna
   go jogging

Lesson 7
It's going to be sunny and warm.

Warm-Up — Look at the weather forecast below and find the correct word from the list for the weather in each day.

Weather	sunny	cloudy	rainy	windy	snowy	foggy
Temperature	hot	warm	cool	cold	dry	humid

WEATHER FORECAST

L: Lowest Temperature
H: Highest Temperature

This Week's Weather

	Weather	Temperature
Monday		cold
Tuesday		cool
Wednesday		cool
Thursday		humid
Friday		warm
Saturday		warm
Sunday		dry

Dialogue — Listen to the dialogue and practice.

Crystal: Oh no!
Andy: What's wrong?
Crystal: Look at the sky. It looks like *it's going to rain soon.* What's the weather forecast for tomorrow?
Andy: Wait, let me check. Hmm…the weather forecast says *it's going to be sunny and warm tomorrow.*
Crystal: Really? That's great!
Andy: Why?
Crystal: Because *I'm going to the beach tomorrow.*
Andy: Great! Have fun!

Comprehension Check!
What does the sky look like now?
What's the weather forecast for tomorrow? | Where is Crystal going tomorrow?

Role-Play
Using the above dialogue, roleplay with your partner using your own personal information.

Grammar Point 1 — Future: Affirmative Statements

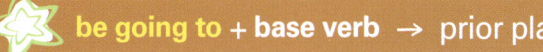 be going to + base verb → prior plans

I **am going to** play baseball on Saturday.   (= I**'m going to** …)
It **is going to** rain next Monday.   (= It**'s going to** …)
We **are going to** take a walk this afternoon.   (= We**'re going to** …)

Lesson 7 · 53

Grammar Point 2 *Future: Negative Statements*

He / She**'s not going to** go shopping tomorrow.　　(= He / She **isn't going to** …)
We**'re not going to** take a walk this afternoon.　　(= We **aren't going to** …)
They**'re not going to** dance the tango in the contest.　　(= They **aren't going to** …)

Practice *Practice the dialogue with a partner. See the example below.*

sunny and warm
go to an amusement park

Example

A: Wow! The weather is lovely today.
B: Yes, it is. I hope it's not going to rain tomorrow.
A: Let me check. The forecast says it's going to be **sunny and warm**. Do you have any plans for tomorrow?
B: Yes, I do. I'm going to **go to an amusement park**.

1
cloudy and humid
go hiking

2
windy and cold
go on picnics

3
rainy and cool
play basketball with my friends

4
snowy and cold
go skiing

5
sunny and dry
go swimming in the ocean

6
cloudy and foggy
invite my friends over to my house

7
windy and dry
go for a drive

8
rainy and humid
clean my house

9
sunny and hot
play tennis

Pair Work

STUDENT A

Divide the class into pairs. One student will be **Student A**, and the other will be **Student B**. Referring to the sample dialogue below, form questions and answers using the information provided.

- 😊 : How's your life these days in **London**?
- 🙂 : Well, I'm enjoying my life here, but the weather here is so unpredictable.
- 😊 : Do you always check the weather forecast?
- 🙂 : Yes, I do.
- 😊 : What will the weather be like next **Monday**?
- 🙂 : It's going to be **cloudy and humid**.
- 😊 : Do you have any plans?
- 🙂 : Well… I'm going to **ride a bicycle in the park**.

1 Ask **Student B** questions about the weather in **Sydney** and his/her plans for next week to complete the chart below.

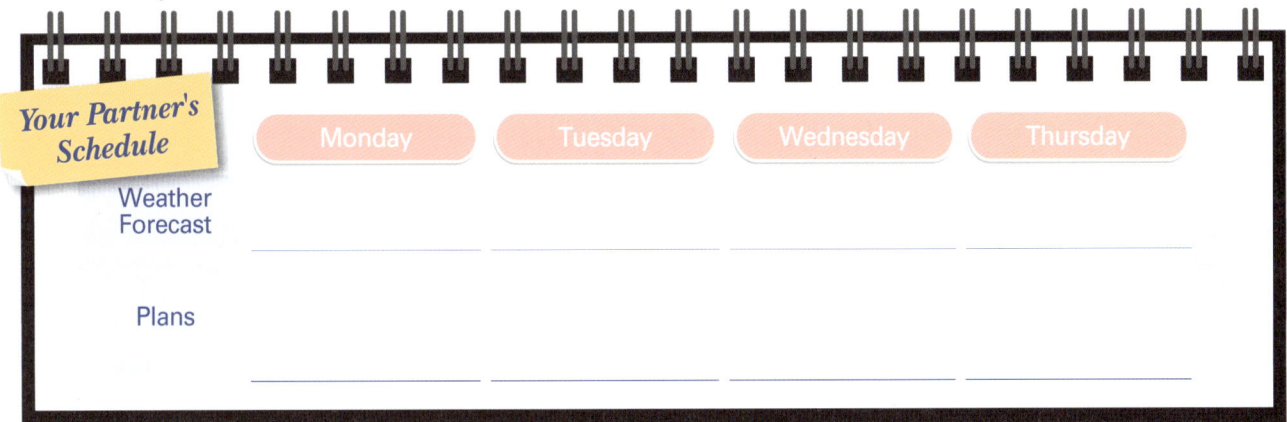

Your Partner's Schedule — Monday | Tuesday | Wednesday | Thursday

Weather Forecast

Plans

2 Imagine you are living in **New York**. Answer **Student B**'s questions by telling him/her about your schedule below.

Your Schedule — Monday | Tuesday | Wednesday | Thursday

Weather Forecast: cold | cool | dry | humid

Plans

Lesson 7 • 55

Pair Work

Divide the class into pairs. One student will be **Student A**, and the other will be **Student B**. Referring to the sample dialogue below, form questions and answers using the information provided.

☺ : How's your life these days in **London**?
☺ : Well, I'm enjoying my life here, but the weather here is so unpredictable.
☺ : Do you always check the weather forecast?
☺ : Yes, I do.
☺ : What will the weather be like next **Monday**?
☺ : It's going to be **cloudy and humid**.
☺ : Do you have any plans?
☺ : Well… I'm going to **ride a bicycle in the park**.

1 Imagine you are living in **Sydney**. Answer **Student A**'s questions by telling him / her about your schedule below.

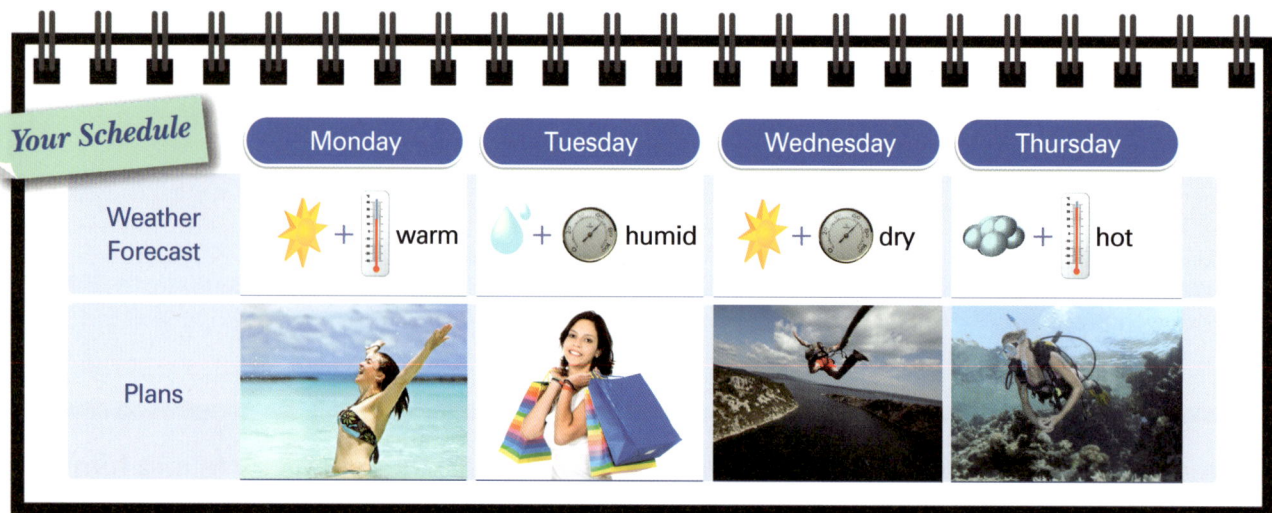

Your Schedule

	Monday	Tuesday	Wednesday	Thursday
Weather Forecast	☀+🌡 warm	💧+🧭 humid	☀+🧭 dry	☁+🌡 hot
Plans				

2 Ask **Student A** questions about the weather in **New York** and his / her plans for next week to complete the chart below.

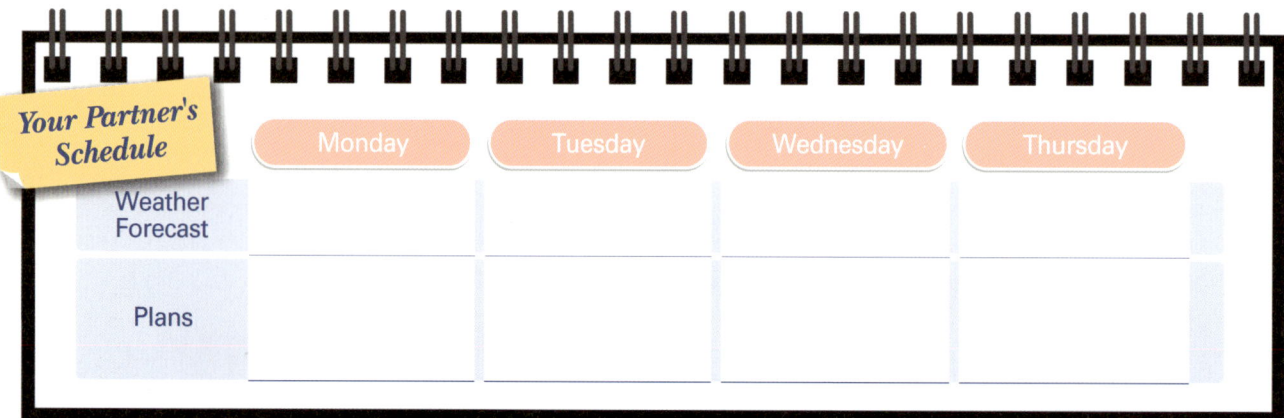

Your Partner's Schedule

	Monday	Tuesday	Wednesday	Thursday
Weather Forecast				
Plans				

Pronunciation

Listen to the following sentences and repeat after them.

1. I'm going to study this weekend.
   I'm not going to study this weekend.

2. It's going to be windy and cold tomorrow.
   It's not going to be windy and cold tomorrow.

3. He's going to go rafting this Saturday.
   She's going to go sailing this Saturday.

4. We're going to invite our friends over to our house.
   You're going to invite your friends over to your house.

5. He's not going to play basketball this afternoon.
   He isn't going to play basketball this afternoon.

6. It's not going to be snowy on Sunday.
   It isn't going to be snowy on Sunday.

Stretch Out!

More Weather Conditions

▶ overcast	▶ partly cloudy	▶ showery	▶ stormy	▶ frosty

It's going to be overcast on Saturday.	It's going to be partly cloudy tomorrow.	It's going to be windy and showery next Tuesday.	It's going to be stormy at night.	It's going to be cold and frosty in the morning.

Lesson 8
How are you going to get there?

Warm-Up Write the names of the transportation into each picture.

– Word List –

bus	subway	(air)plane	boat
motorbike	taxi	truck	train
car	express bus	high-speed rail	bicycle

I'm going to get there by…

🎧 Dialogue — Listen to the dialogue and practice.

Gary: *What are you going to do for winter vacation?*
Eunice: Hmm… I'm going to go to Florida with my family. I'm so excited!
Gary: Oh, really? *How are you going to get there?*
Eunice: We're going to get there by plane.
Gary: Wow! I envy you so much. *Are you going to stay there for the entire vacation?*
Eunice: No, we're not. Only for a week.
Gary: Oh, I see. Have a safe trip.

Comprehension Check!
Where is Eunice going? | Who is Eunice going with?
Is Eunice going there by express bus? | How long is Eunice going to stay there?

Role-Play
Using the above dialogue, roleplay with your partner using your own personal information.

Grammar Point 1 — Future: Yes/No Questions

Yes / No Questions	Short Answers	
Are you going to have a barbecue party?	Yes, I **am**.	No, I**'m not**.
Is he/she going to visit his/her cousin?	Yes, he/she **is**.	No, he/she**'s not**. (= **isn't**)
Are we going (to go)* to a soccer game?	Yes, we **are**.	No, we**'re not**.
Are you going to play basketball?	Yes, we **are**.	No, we**'re not**.
Are they going to throw a housewarming party?	Yes, they **are**.	No, they**'re not**.

* I**'m going** to the beach now. → Now
  I**'m going to go** to the beach this weekend. → Future (Plan)
  = I**'m going** to the beach this weekend.

Lesson 8 · 59

Grammar Point 2 Future: Wh-questions

Wh-questions	Answers
What are you going to do during your vacation?	**I'm going to** practice driving.
What is he / she going to do tomorrow?	**He / She's going to** have a blind date.
What are we going to have for dinner?	**We're going to** have Chinese food for dinner.
What are you going to have for lunch?	**We're going to** have pizza for lunch.
What are they going to eat?	**They're going to** eat Korean food.
How long are you going to stay there?	**I'm going to** stay there for three months.

Practice Practice the dialogue with a partner. See the example below.

Valentine's Day

take my girlfriend to a fancy restaurant
car / give her a present

Example

A: Do you have any plans for <u>Valentine's Day</u>?
B: Yes, I do. I'm going to <u>take my girlfriend to a fancy restaurant</u>.
A: Oh, really? How are you going to get there?
B: We're going to get there by <u>car</u>.
A: What are you going to do?
B: Well… I'm going to <u>give her a present</u>.

① Christmas Day

visit my family back home
express bus / spend time with my family

② your birthday

celebrate my birthday on the beach
car / have a barbecue party with my friends

③ New Year's Eve

watch fireworks
subway / make New Year's resolutions

④ Halloween

go to a club
taxi / dance at a party

Pair Work

 **STUDENT A**

Divide the class into pairs. One student will be **Student A**, and the other will be **Student B**. Referring to the sample dialogue below, form questions and answers using the information provided.

☺ : Where is Jennifer going this weekend?
☺ : She's going to the east coast with her friends.
☺ : How is she going to get there?
☺ : I think she's going to get there by high-speed rail.
☺ : I see. What is she going to do on the east coast?
☺ : She's going to play beach volleyball.

1 Match the names with the pictures by asking **Student B** questions.

Crystal
Danny
Nicole
Ken

2 Answer **Student B**'s questions, referring to the information below.

	Where	How	What
Robert	Mission Bay	bicycle	play ball games on the beach
Monica	Bondi Beach	express bus	swim in the ocean
Jay	west coast	motorbike	watch fireworks on the beach
Sue	Long Island	plane	travel around the island

Lesson 8 · 61

Pair Work

STUDENT B

Divide the class into pairs. One student will be **Student A**, and the other will be **Student B**. Referring to the sample dialogue below, form questions and answers using the information provided.

☺ : Where is Jennifer going this weekend?
☺ : She's going to the east coast with her friends.
☺ : How is she going to get there?
☺ : I think she's going to get there by high-speed rail.
☺ : I see. What is she going to do on the east coast?
☺ : She's going to play beach volleyball.

1 Answer **Student A**'s questions, referring to the information below.

	Where	How	What
Crystal	South Bay	boat	have a barbecue party
Danny	Palm Beach	car	go surfing
Nicole	Miami Beach	high-speed rail	get a suntan
Ken	Hilton Beach	bus	go sailing

2 Match the names with the pictures by asking **Student A** questions.

Robert
Monica
Jay
Sue

Pronunciation
Listen to the following sentences and repeat after them.

1. Are you going to make some cookies this weekend?
   Are you gonna make some cookies this weekend?

> In informal speech, people usually say /gənə/ (gonna), instead of "going to".

2. Are we going to have lunch together tomorrow?
   Are we gonna have lunch together tomorrow?

3. Is he going to look around town on Saturday?
   Is he gonna look around town on Saturday?

4. What is she going to do for winter vacation?
   What is she gonna do for winter vacation?

5. What are you going to have for dinner?
   What are you gonna have for dinner?

6. How long are they going to stay at their grandma's?
   How long are they gonna stay at their grandma's?

Stretch Out!

More Transportation Words

bus stop   taxi stand   train station   subway station   dock   airport

Lesson 9 — What will you do next year?

Warm-Up Complete the sentences, using the appropriate expressions.

— Expressions —

get a promotion	win the lottery	go abroad	go on a date
become famous	make foreign friends	get married	get a job
become a millionaire	find his true love	have a baby	

He will _____.

They will _____.

He will _____.

They will _____.

He will _____.

He will _____.

She will _____.

You will _____.

She will _____.

They will _____.

He will _____.

Dialogue *Listen to the dialogue and practice.*

Peter: Katie, what are you doing?
Katie: I'm writing my plans for next year.
Peter: Wow! So, what are your plans? *What will you do next year?*
Katie: Well… *I will go abroad and make many foreign friends.* And *I will enter a graduate school there.* What about you, Peter?
Peter: *I hope I'll find my true love and get married next year.* Those are my plans and my wishes at the same time.
Katie: I hope they will come true.

Comprehension Check!
What are Katie's plans for next year?
What will Peter do next year?

Role-Play
Using the above dialogue, roleplay with your partner using your own personal information.

Grammar Point 1 *Future: Affirmative / Negative Statements*

will + base verb → promises, decisions, predictions

	Affirmative Statements	Negative Statements
Promises	I **will** be on time. (= I**'ll** be on time.)	I **will not** be on time. (= I **won't** be on time.)
Decisions	I **will** meet my friends this weekend. (= I**'ll** meet my friends this weekend.)	I **will not** meet my friends this weekend. (= I **won't** meet my friends this weekend.)
Predictions	You **will** get married in three years.	You **will not** get married in three years. (= You **won't** get married in three years.)

Lesson 9 • 65

Grammar Point 2 *Future: Questions*

Yes / No Questions	Wh-Questions
Will he play soccer this Saturday? **Yes**, he **will**. **No**, he **will not**. (= No, he **won't**.) **Will** they get married next year? **Yes**, they **will**. **No**, they **will not**. (= No, they **won't**.)	**What will** you buy? **I'll** buy some clothes. **When will** you leave? **I'll** leave tomorrow. **Where will** he stay? **He'll** stay at his uncle's (house). **How long will** they stay there? **They'll** stay there for two months.

Practice *Practice the dialogue with a partner. See the example below.*

relax at home

see a rock concert

Example

A: Do you have any plans for the holiday?
B: Not yet. I think I'll just <u>relax at home</u>. How about you?
A: I'm going to <u>see a rock concert</u>. Do you want to come? I'm sure you will enjoy it!
B: <u>A rock concert</u>? Okay, I'll go with you, then.

clean the house

see a musical performance

watch DVDs at home

have a barbecue party at my place

take a walk in the park

play soccer

ride a bicycle around town

go shopping at the mall

Pair Work

STUDENT A

Divide the class into pairs. One student will be **Student A**, and the other will be **Student B**.
Referring to the sample dialogue below, form questions and answers using the information provided.

😊 : Will <u>Susan go on a date</u>?
🙂 : Yes, <u>she</u> will.
😊 : Will <u>she go on a date</u> in <u>a month</u>?
🙂 : Yes, <u>she</u> will. .... end
　　No, <u>she</u> won't. .... continue
😊 : Then when will <u>she ever go on a date</u>?
🙂 : <u>She'll go on a date</u> in <u>five months</u>.
😊 : Oh, I see.

1 Ask **Student B** questions about Jenny's future.

2 Answer **Student B**'s questions about Paul's future.

Pair Work

Divide the class into pairs. One student will be **Student A**, and the other will be **Student B**. Referring to the sample dialogue below, form questions and answers using the information provided.

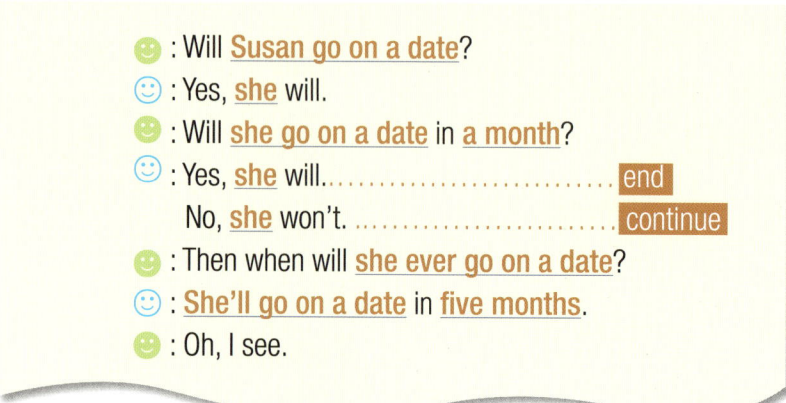

☺ : Will Susan go on a date?
☺ : Yes, she will.
☺ : Will she go on a date in a month?
☺ : Yes, she will. .... end
   No, she won't. .... continue
☺ : Then when will she ever go on a date?
☺ : She'll go on a date in five months.
☺ : Oh, I see.

Right ☐ Wrong ☐

1 Answer **Student A**'s questions about Jenny's future.

2 Ask **Student A** questions about Paul's future.

Right ☐ Wrong ☐   Right ☐ Wrong ☐   Right ☐ Wrong ☐   Right ☐ Wrong ☐

Pronunciation Listen to the following sentences and repeat after them.

1. I **will** visit you tomorrow.
   I **won't** visit you tomorrow.

2. She **will** probably go shopping this weekend.
   She**'ll** probably go shopping this weekend.

3. You will get a job **in three months**.
   You will get a job **in three years**.

4. Will I **find my true love** this year?
   Will I **win the lottery** this year?

5. What will **you do** in the future?
   What will **I become** in the future?

6. When will he **arrive**?
   Where will he **stay**?

Stretch Out!

More Fortune Telling

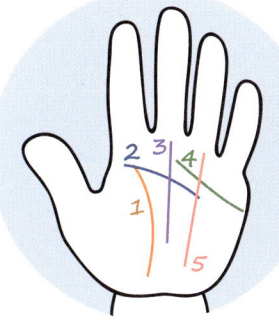

Palm Reading

1. Life Line — long – You will live a long life.
2. Head Line — long – You will be intelligent.
3. Fate Line — deep – Your life will be controlled by fate.
4. Heart Line — single line – You will have one romance.
5. Success Line — deep – You will be successful in what you do.

Lesson 10: I'd like to book a flight to New York.

Warm-Up *Match the words with the pictures.*

– Word List –

first class   a one-way ticket   business class   a window seat
an aisle seat   economy class   a round-trip ticket

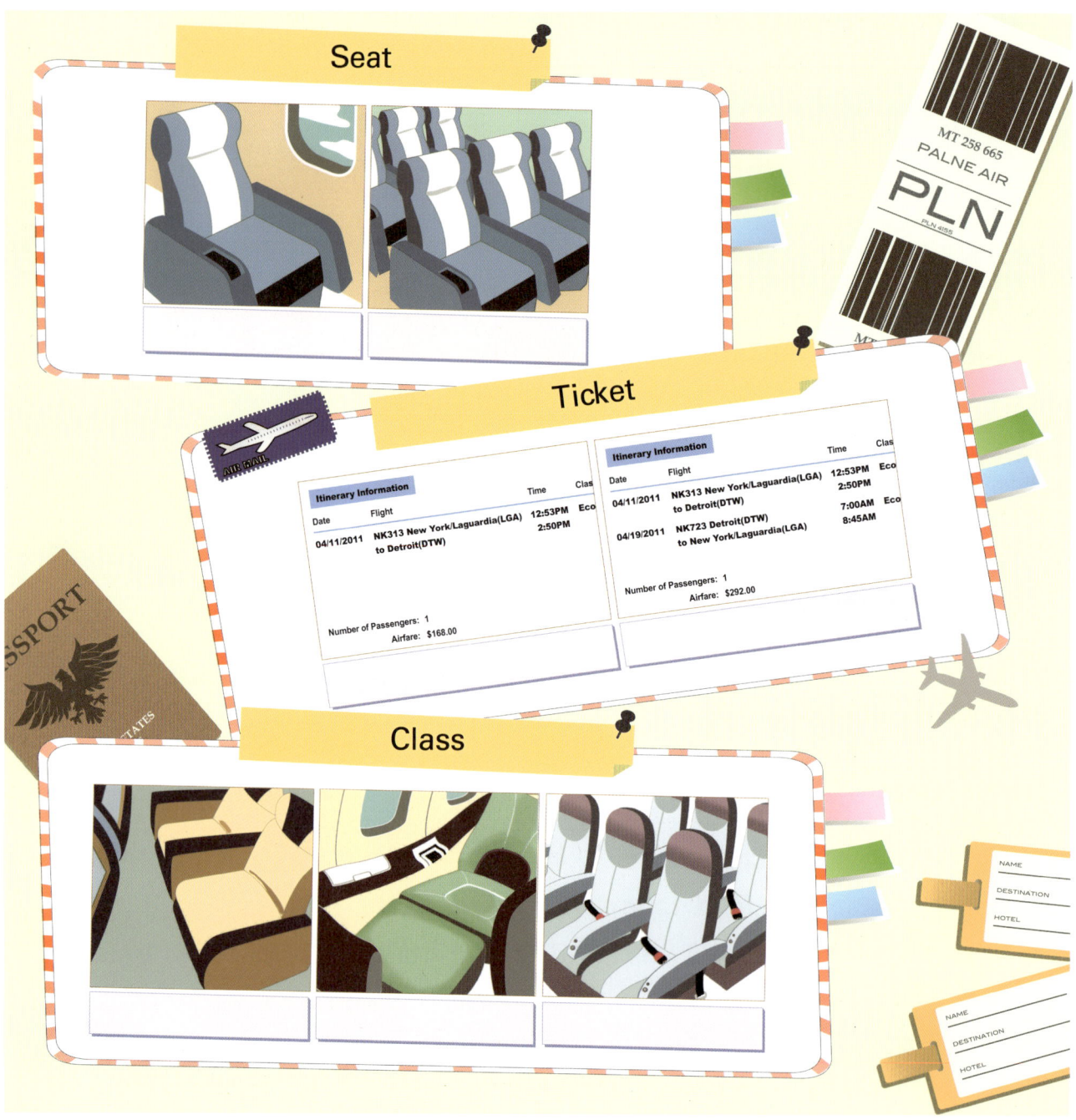

Dialogue — Listen to the dialogue and practice.

Receptionist: United Airlines. How can I help you?
Sandra: **I'd like to book a flight to New York.**
Receptionist: OK. **When would you like to leave?**
Sandra: This coming Sunday morning.
Receptionist: OK. Hold on please. (pause) We have one at 9 a.m.
Sandra: Oh, good. I will take it.

Comprehension Check!
Why did Sandra make the call?
When does Sandra want to leave?

Role-Play
Using the above dialogue, roleplay with your partner using your own personal information.

Grammar Point — Would like to vs. Would like

Questions	Answers
How may I help you?	I **would like to** book a flight to London. (= I**'d like to** book a flight to London.)
When **would** you **like to** leave?	I **would like to** leave on July 5th. (= I**'d like to** leave on July 5th.)
Which class **would** you **like to** fly in?	I **would like to** fly in economy class. (= I**'d like to** fly in economy class.)
Would you **like** a window or an aisle seat?	I **would like** an aisle seat, please. (= I**'d like** an aisle seat, please.)

Practice
Practice the dialogue with a partner. See the example below.

Seoul
Saturday 10 a.m.

Example

A: Pacific Airlines. How can I help you?
B: I'd like to book a flight to Seoul.
A: Ok. When would you like to leave?
B: I'd like to leave on Saturday.
A: We have a flight leaving at 10 a.m.
B: Oh, good. I'll take it.

1. Los Angeles — Saturday 6 p.m.
2. London — Tuesday 2 a.m.
3. Hong Kong — Friday 9 a.m.
4. Sydney — Monday 11 a.m.
5. Cairo — Wednesday 3 a.m.
6. Brasilia — Thursday 10 p.m.

STUDENT A

Divide the class into pairs. One student will be **Student A**, and the other will be **Student B**. Referring to the sample dialogue below, form questions and answers using the information provided.

☺ : International Airlines. How may I help you?
☺ : I'd like to reserve <u>a one-way ticket</u> to <u>Paris</u>.
☺ : When would you like to leave?
☺ : I'd like to leave on <u>June 24th</u>.
☺ : Which class would you like to fly in?
☺ : I'd like to fly in <u>business class</u>.
☺ : Would you like a window or an aisle seat?
☺ : <u>An aisle seat</u>, please.

1 Fill in the boxes with information about the flights you want to book.

	Ticket	Destination	Departure Date	Class	Seat
01	a round-trip ticket			business class	
02		Singapore			an aisle seat
03			February 12th		a window seat

2 Ask **Student B** questions about his / her flight information and fill in the blanks.

	Ticket	Destination	Departure Date	Class	Seat
01					
02					
03					

Lesson 10 · 73

Pair Work

STUDENT B

Divide the class into pairs. One student will be **Student A**, and the other will be **Student B**. Referring to the sample dialogue below, form questions and answers using the information provided.

- 🙂 : International Airlines. How may I help you?
- 🙂 : I'd like to reserve <u>a one-way ticket</u> to <u>Paris</u>.
- 🙂 : When would you like to leave?
- 🙂 : I'd like to leave on <u>June 24th</u>.
- 🙂 : Which class would you like to fly in?
- 🙂 : I'd like to fly in <u>business class</u>.
- 🙂 : Would you like a window or an aisle seat?
- 🙂 : <u>An aisle seat</u>, please.

1 Fill in the boxes with information about the flights you want to book.

	Ticket	Destination	Departure Date	Class	Seat
01			July 9th		an aisle seat
02	a round-trip ticket			economy class	
03	a one-way ticket	Hawaii			

2 Ask **Student A** questions about his / her flight information and fill in the blanks.

	Ticket	Destination	Departure Date	Class	Seat
01					
02					
03					

Pronunciation
Listen to the following sentences and repeat after them.

1. Would you like an aisle seat?
   Would you like a window seat?

2. I'd like to fly in first class.
   I'd like to fly in economy class.

3. I would like to reserve a flight to Los Angeles.
   I'd like to reserve a flight to Los Angeles.

4. I'd like a one-way ticket to Sydney.
   I'd like a round-trip ticket to Sydney.

5. Would you like to book business class?
   Would you like to book economy class?

Stretch Out!

More Expressions for Flights

- When should I check in?
- When is boarding time?
- Which is our boarding gate?
- Which airport do I leave from?
- Could you tell me my reservation number?
- What is the flight number and departure time?
- How much is the fare from Chicago to New York?

Lesson 10 · 75

Lesson 11
May I take your order?

Warm-Up Complete the menu using the appropriate words from the list.

– Word List –

| Desserts | Steak | Pie | Salmon | Appetizers |
| Salad | Soup | Chocolate | Main Dishes | Chicken |

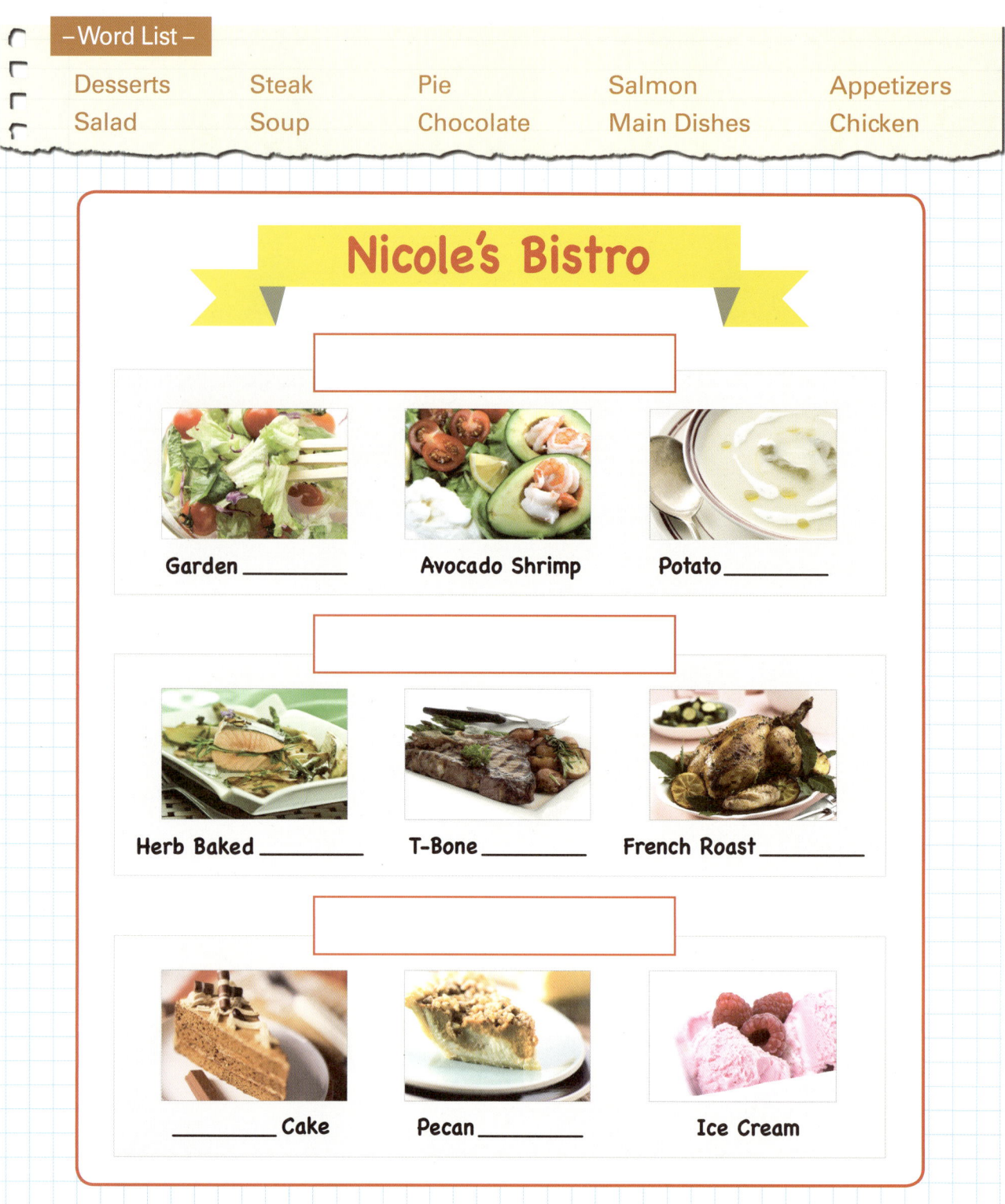

Nicole's Bistro

_____

- Garden _____
- Avocado Shrimp
- Potato _____

_____

- Herb Baked _____
- T-Bone _____
- French Roast _____

_____

- _____ Cake
- Pecan _____
- Ice Cream

Dialogue — Listen to the dialogue and practice.

Waiter: *May I take your order?*
Mandy: Yes, please.
I'd like the salmon salad for an appetizer.
Waiter: And what would you like to have for the main dish?
Mandy: I'll have the rib-eye steak. I'd like my steak medium well done.
Waiter: Anything else?
Mandy: *Could I have the ice cream for dessert?*
Waiter: Sure. What flavor would you like?
Mandy: Chocolate, please.

Comprehension Check!
What appetizer does Mandy want?
What main dish does Mandy choose? | What dessert is Mandy going to have?

Role-Play
Using the above dialogue, roleplay with your partner using your own personal information.

Grammar Point — Modals: May, Could, Can

	Asking for Permission	
Formal	**May I** take your order?	Yes, please.
		Just a moment, please.
↓	**Could I** have some wine, please?	Yes, of course.
		I'm sorry, but we don't serve alcohol here.
Informal	**Can I** have soup for an appetizer?	Certainly.
		Sorry, but we only serve salad for an appetizer.

Practice — Practice the dialogue with a partner. See the example below.

avocado shrimp
T-bone steak
chocolate cake

 Example

A: May I take your order?
B: Yes, please. I'll have the <u>avocado shrimp</u> for an appetizer.
A: And what would you like for the main dish?
B: I'll have the <u>T-bone steak</u>.
A: Anything else?
B: Could I have the <u>chocolate cake</u> for dessert?
A: Certainly.

1
mushroom soup
grilled chicken
carrot cake

2
fried cheese
roast beef
cheesecake

3
potato soup
baked salmon
apple pie

4
chicken wings
rib-eye steak
pudding

5
salmon salad
roast turkey
ice cream

6
garden salad
smoked tuna
pecan pie

STUDENT A

Divide the class into pairs. One student will be **Student A**, and the other will be **Student B**. Referring to the sample dialogue below, form questions and answers using the information provided.

- 😊 : Good evening. May I take your order?
- 🙂 : Yes. Could I have the **salmon salad** for an appetizer?
- 😊 : Sure. And for the main dish?
- 🙂 : I'll have the **grilled chicken**. And can I have the **cheesecake** for dessert?
- 😊 : Certainly. Anything to drink?
- 🙂 : A glass of red wine, please.

MENU

Appetizers

Garden Salad	Salmon Salad
Potato Soup	Mushroom Soup
Avocado Shrimp	Fried Cheese

Main Dishes

Baked Salmon	Grilled Chicken
T-Bone Steak	Rib-Eye Steak
Roast Turkey	Smoked Tuna

Desserts

Ice Cream	Pudding
Apple Pie	Cheesecake
Carrot Cake	Pecan Pie

1 Decide what you are going to order. Make three choices for each category.

Your Choices

	Appetizers	Main Dishes	Desserts
1.			
2.			
3.			

2 Ask **Student B** what he/she is going to order and fill in the blanks.

Your Partner's Choices

	Appetizers	Main Dishes	Desserts
1.			
2.			
3.			

Lesson 11 · 79

Pair Work

STUDENT B

Divide the class into pairs. One student will be **Student A**, and the other will be **Student B**. Referring to the sample dialogue below, form questions and answers using the information provided.

- : Good evening. May I take your order?
- : Yes. Could I have the <u>salmon salad</u> for an appetizer?
- : Sure. And for the main dish?
- : I'll have the <u>grilled chicken</u>. And can I have the <u>cheesecake</u> for dessert?
- : Certainly. Anything to drink?
- : A glass of red wine, please.

MENU

Appetizers

Garden Salad	Salmon Salad
Potato Soup	Mushroom Soup
Avocado Shrimp	Fried Cheese

Main Dishes

Baked Salmon	Grilled Chicken
T-Bone Steak	Rib-Eye Steak
Roast Turkey	Smoked Tuna

Desserts

Ice Cream	Pudding
Apple Pie	Cheesecake
Carrot Cake	Pecan pie

1 Decide what you are going to order. Make three choices for each category.

Your Choices

	Appetizers	Main Dishes	Desserts
1.			
2.			
3.			

2 Ask **Student A** what he/she is going to order and fill in the blanks.

Your Partner's Choices

	Appetizers	Main Dishes	Desserts
1.			
2.			
3.			

Pronunciation Listen to the following sentences and repeat after them.

1. **Can** I have the mushroom soup for an appetizer?
   Could I have the mushroom soup for an appetizer?

2. Can I have the **cheesecake** for dessert?
   Can I have the **chocolate cake** for dessert?

3. **May** I have a glass of red wine?
   Can I have a glass of red wine?

4. Can I have the **T-bone steak** for my main dish?
   Can I have the **Rib-eye steak** for my main dish?

5. **Could** I have the salmon salad for an appetizer?
   May I have the salmon salad for an appetizer?

Stretch Out!

More Expressions for Restaurants

- I'd like to reserve a table for five people.
- Will you check my order?
- How long do we have to wait to order?

- Would you bring me the menu, please?
- What's today's special?
- What's the chef's recommendation?

- What kind of dressing do you have?
- I'd like my steak rare / medium well done / well done.
- This is too salty / spicy / greasy / sour / sweet.

- The check, please.
- Could you bring me the bill?

Lesson 12

You should see a doctor.

Warm-Up What should you do and what shouldn't you do when you have the health problems below? Complete the sentences using **should** or **shouldn't**.

earache	She _____ listen to loud music.	
cold / flu	He _____ go home and rest.	
stomachache	She _____ (go) see a doctor.	
headache	He _____ take some medicine.	
backache	She _____ exercise so much.	
toothache	He _____ go to the dentist.	
fever	She _____ drink alcohol.	
sore throat	He _____ drink hot tea.	
sore eyes	She _____ wear contact lens.	

Dialogue  *Listen to the dialogue and practice.*

Kelly: James, what's wrong? You don't look well.
James: Hey, Kelly. I have a sore throat.
Kelly: There's a bad flu going around. *You should see a doctor.*
James: Maybe later.
Kelly: *You have to go see a doctor right away.* Promise me you will go asap.
James: All right. I promise.

Comprehension Check!
What's wrong with James?
What should James do?

Role-Play
Using the above dialogue, roleplay with your partner using your own personal information.

Grammar Point — Modals: Should & Have to

	should (giving advice)	have to (expressing necessity)
Positive	You **should** exercise regularly.	We **have to** drink hot tea. He **has to** go home and rest.
Negative	You **shouldn't** use contact lens.	They **don't have to** go to the dentist. She **doesn't have to** take any medicine.

Practice
Practice the dialogue with a partner. See the example below.

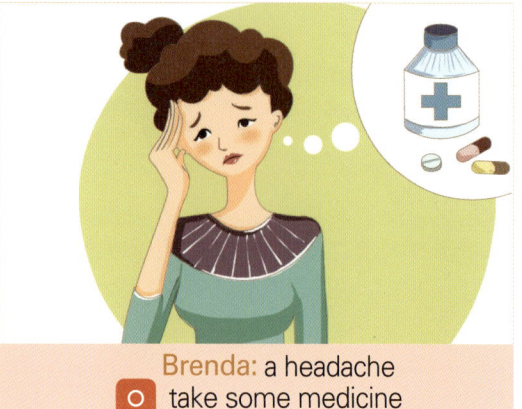

Brenda: a headache
○ take some medicine

Example

A: <u>Brenda</u> looks terrible. What's the matter with her?
B: <u>She</u> has <u>a headache</u>.
A: <u>She</u> should (has to) <u>take some medicine</u>.
B: I'll talk to <u>her</u> about it.

❶ Jason: a cold
○ go home and rest

❷ Sarah: sore eyes
✗ wear contact lens

❸ Jeremy: a backache
✗ exercise so much

❹ Jessica: a toothache
○ go see a dentist

❺ Patrick: an earache
✗ listen to loud music

❻ Pam: a sore throat
○ drink hot tea

STUDENT A

Divide the class into pairs. One student will be **Student A**, and the other will be **Student B**. Referring to the sample dialogue below, share your ideas with your partner.

☺ : I'm not feeling good. I have <u>a fever</u>.
☺ : You <u>should (have to) go home and rest</u>.
☺ : Ok. I'll do that.
☺ : And remember, you <u>shouldn't drink alcohol</u>.
☺ : Ok. I'll keep that in mind.
☺ : Hope you feel better soon.
☺ : Thanks a lot.

1 Fill in the boxes with what the people *should* or *shouldn't* do.

	should / have to	shouldn't
a cold		
a backache		
a stomachache		
sore eyes		

2 Ask **Student B** what you *should* or *shouldn't* do in the situations below.

a headache | a toothache | an earache | a sore throat

Pair Work

 **STUDENT B**

Divide the class into pairs. One student will be **Student A**, and the other will be **Student B**. Referring to the sample dialogue below, share your ideas with your partner.

☺ : I'm not feeling good. I have a fever.
☺ : You should (have to) go home and rest.
☺ : Ok. I'll do that.
☺ : And remember, you shouldn't drink alcohol.
☺ : Ok. I'll keep that in mind.
☺ : Hope you feel better soon.
☺ : Thanks a lot.

1 Fill in the boxes with what the people *should* or *shouldn't* do.

	should / have to	shouldn't
a headache		
a toothache		
an earache		
a sore throat		

2 Ask **Student A** what you *should* or *shouldn't* do in the situations below.

a cold   a backache   a stomachache   sore eyes

Pronunciation Listen to the following sentences and repeat after them.

1 I have a terrible stomachache.
I have a terrible toothache.

2 You should take some medicine.
You shouldn't take any medicine.

3 We have to exercise regularly.
He has to exercise regularly.

4 She has a sore throat.
She has sore eyes.

5 They don't have to go to the dentist.
He doesn't have to go to the dentist.

Stretch Out!

More Expressions for Health

Q What should we do to stay healthy?
= What do we have to do to stay healthy?

- We should / have to avoid stress.
- We should / have to eat a proper diet.
- We should / have to stay physically fit.
- We should / have to drink lots of water.
- We should / have to have a positive mind.

Q What shouldn't we do to stay healthy?

- We shouldn't skip meals.
- We shouldn't drink and smoke.
- We shouldn't eat snacks late at night.
- We shouldn't consume too much salt.
- We shouldn't have a negative mind.

Lesson 13: The gold ring is prettier than the silver one.

Warm-Up Choose the correct option for each picture.

Stella is (**thinner / fatter**) than Derek.

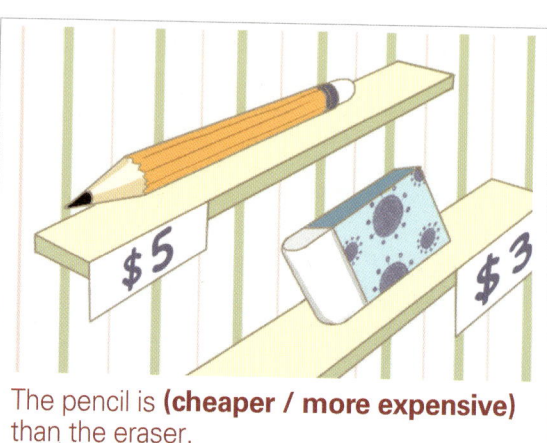
The pencil is (**cheaper / more expensive**) than the eraser.

The car is (**larger / smaller**) than the van.

The silver purse is (**prettier / uglier**) than the brown one.

Carlos is (**taller / shorter**) than Amanda.

High heels are (**less comfortable / more comfortable**) than sneakers.

Dialogue *Listen to the dialogue and practice.*

Ken: So, which ring do you like?
Nicole: I can't choose between these two.
Ken: Hmm. Which one is prettier?
Nicole: **The gold ring is prettier than the silver one.**
Ken: Then, let's get that one.
Nicole: **But it's more expensive.**
Ken: Don't you worry about it.
Nicole: Oh, you're so sweet.

Comprehension Check!
Which ring is prettier? | Which ring is more expensive?

Role-Play
Using the above dialogue, roleplay with your partner using your own personal information.

Grammar Point *Comparatives*

adjective + er	Sarah is **taller than** Erica. Erica is **shorter than** Sarah.
more / less + adjective	The blue pen is **more expensive than** the red one. The red pen is **less expensive than** the blue one.
irregular	Mary's English is **better than** mine. My English is **worse than** Mary's.

Point!

large → large**r**	fat → fat**ter**	pretty → prett**ier**
cute → cute**r**	big → big**ger**	ugly → ugl**ier**

Lesson 13 • 89

Practice
Practice the dialogue with a partner. See the example below.

suit / cheap

Example
A: Do you like this **black suit**?
B: Not really. I think **the blue one** is better than **the black one**.
A: Why?
B: It's **cheaper**.

pants / cheap

Example
A: Do you like these **black pants**?
B: Not really. I think **the blue ones** are better than **the black ones**.
A: Why?
B: They're **cheaper**.

1. umbrella / big
2. purse / small
3. dress / expensive
4. shorts / short
5. shoes / pretty
6. jacket / comfortable

STUDENT A

Divide the class into pairs. One student will be **Student A**, and the other will be **Student B**. Referring to the sample dialogue below, form questions and answers using the information provided.

☺ : Which one is <u>Lisa</u>?
☺ : Take a guess.
☺ : Is <u>she taller</u> than <u>Emma</u>?
☺ : Yes, <u>she</u> is. <u>She</u> is <u>taller</u> than <u>Emma</u>.
☺ : Then, <u>she</u> must be <u>Lisa</u>.
☺ : That's correct.

☺ : Which one is <u>Alex</u>?
☺ : Take a guess.
☺ : Is <u>he thinner</u> than <u>Joshua</u>?
☺ : No, <u>he</u> isn't. <u>He</u> isn't <u>thinner</u> than <u>Joshua</u>.
☺ : Then, <u>he</u> must be <u>Alex</u>.
☺ : That's correct.

1 Match the names with the pictures by asking **Student B** questions.

2 Answer **Student B**'s questions about the people in the picture.

Pair Work

STUDENT B

Divide the class into pairs. One student will be **Student A**, and the other will be **Student B**. Referring to the sample dialogue below, form questions and answers using the information provided.

- 😊 : Which one is <u>Lisa</u>?
- ☺ : Take a guess.
- 😊 : Is <u>she taller</u> than <u>Emma</u>?
- ☺ : Yes, <u>she</u> is. <u>She</u> is <u>taller</u> than <u>Emma</u>.
- 😊 : Then, <u>she</u> must be <u>Lisa</u>.
- ☺ : That's correct.

- 😊 : Which one is <u>Alex</u>?
- ☺ : Take a guess.
- 😊 : Is <u>he thinner</u> than <u>Joshua</u>?
- ☺ : No, <u>he</u> isn't. <u>He</u> isn't <u>thinner</u> than <u>Joshua</u>.
- 😊 : Then, <u>he</u> must be <u>Alex</u>.
- ☺ : That's correct.

1 Match the names with the pictures by asking *Student A* questions.

2 Answer *Student A*'s questions about the people in the picture.

Pronunciation Listen to the following sentences and repeat after them.

1 He is thinner than her.
She is fatter than him.

2 The pink shirt is prettier than the green one.
The green shirt is uglier than the pink one.

3 This dress is more comfortable than that one.
That dress is less comfortable than this one.

4 My brother is shorter than my sister.
My sister is taller than my brother.

5 Which one is more expensive?
Which ones are more expensive?

Stretch Out!

More Comparatives

- light → lighter
- wise → wiser
- hot → hotter

- delicious → more delicious
- handsome → more handsome
- interesting → more interesting

- dry → drier
- busy → busier
- heavy → heavier

- little → less
- many → more
- much → more

Lesson 13 · 93

Lesson 14 — He's the funniest guy in the company.

Warm-Up Write the adjectives in the correct categories.

– Adjectives –

rude	sad	lazy	selfish
happy	nice	funny	outgoing
friendly	quiet	talkative	hardworking

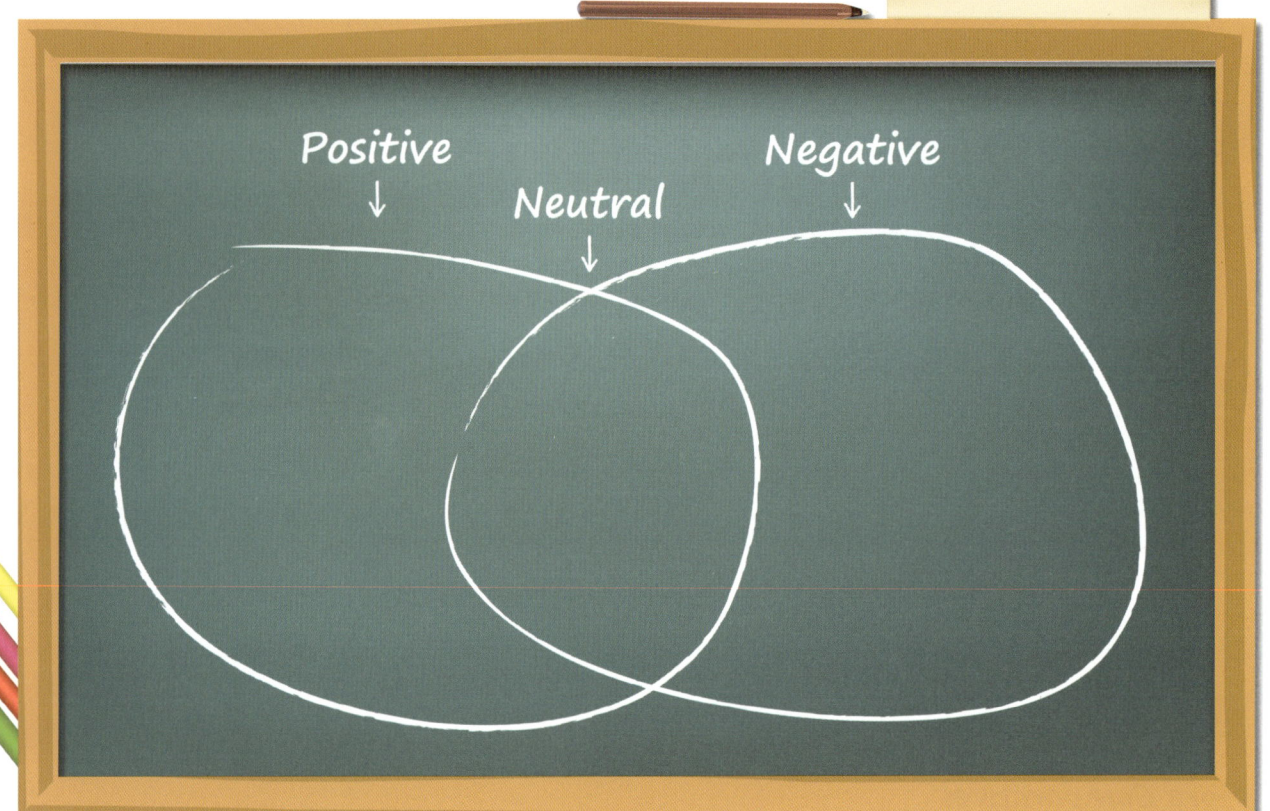

◆ Write the superlative forms of the adjectives below.

friendly → the ___friendliest___   talkative → the _____
quiet → the _____   sad → the _____
lazy → the _____   rude → the _____
selfish → the _____   outgoing → the _____
happy → the _____   funny → the _____
nice → the _____   hardworking → the _____

Dialogue Listen to the dialogue and practice.

Jessica: Do you know Scott, the new guy in our department?
Carlos: No, I don't. What's he like?
Jessica: **He's the funniest guy in the company.** He makes people laugh all the time.
Carlos: What about the new girl in your department? You had two new people, right?
Jessica: Oh, you mean Alicia? **She is the most outgoing person in our department.** She gets along well with everyone.
Carlos: I can't wait to meet them.

Comprehension Check!
What's Scott like? | What's Alicia like?

Role-Play
Using the above dialogue, roleplay with your partner using your own personal information.

Grammar Point — Superlatives

the + adjective + est	Erin is **the quietest** person in the class.
the most + adjective	Nicole is **the most hardworking** person in the company.
irregular	Brad is **the best** employee in the department. Angela is **the worst** employee in the department.

⭐ Point!

nice → nic**est**   sad → sad**dest**   friendly → friend**liest**

Practice Practice the dialogue with a partner. See the example below.

funny / company

outgoing / company

 Example
- A: Do you know **Jerry**?
- B: No, I don't. What's **he** like?
- A: **He**'s very **funny**. **He**'s **the funniest** person in the **company**.
- B: Oh, I cant wait to meet **him**.

 Example
- A: Do you know **Ben and Erica**?
- B: No, I don't. What are **they** like?
- A: **They**'re very **outgoing**. **They**'re **the most outgoing** people in the **company**.
- B: Oh, I can't wait to meet **them**.

❶
nice / office

❷
talkative / class

❸
happy / company

❹
selfish / company

❺
hardworking / class

❻
lazy / office

STUDENT A

Divide the class into pairs. One student will be **Student A**, and the other will be **Student B**. Referring to the sample dialogue below, form questions and answers using the information provided.

😀 : Who is the most talkative person in the class?
🙂 : I think Julie is the most talkative.
😀 : Then, who is the quietest person in the class?
🙂 : I think Carlos is the quietest.

continue

talkative

quiet

1 Decide who in your class best matches the adjectives below and fill in their names.

I think ...

Adjectives	Names	Adjectives	Names
friendly		talkative	
selfish		nice	
funny		hardworking	

2 Ask **Student B** questions to complete the table below.

My partner thinks ...

Adjectives	Names	Adjectives	Names
happy		outgoing	
rude		lazy	
quiet		sad	

Pair Work

STUDENT B

Divide the class into pairs. One student will be **Student A**, and the other will be **Student B**. Referring to the sample dialogue below, form questions and answers using the information provided.

😀 : Who is the most talkative person in the class?
🙂 : I think Julie is the most talkative.
😀 : Then, who is the quietest person in the class?
🙂 : I think Carlos is the quietest.
continue

talkative

quiet

1 Decide who in your class best matches the adjectives below and fill in their names.

I think ...

Adjectives	Names	Adjectives	Names
happy		outgoing	
rude		lazy	
quiet		sad	

2 Ask Student A questions to complete the table below.

My partner thinks ...

Adjectives	Names	Adjectives	Names
friendly		talkative	
selfish		nice	
funny		hardworking	

Pronunciation — Listen to the following sentences and repeat after them.

1. Angela is the rudest girl in the department.
   Angela is the nicest girl in the department.

2. You are the laziest person in the class.
   You are the friendliest person in the class.

3. Carlos is the happiest guy in our company.
   Carlos is the funniest guy in our company.

4. Jane is the most outgoing person in the class.
   Jane is the most hardworking person in the class.

5. He is the best employee in the department.
   She is the worst employee in the department.

Stretch Out!

More Superlatives

- light → lighter → lightest
- wise → wiser → wisest
- hot → hotter → hottest

- delicious → more delicious → most delicious
- handsome → more handsome → most handsome
- interesting → more interesting → most interesting

- dry → drier → driest
- busy → busier → busiest
- heavy → heavier → heaviest

- little → less → least
- many → more → most
- much → more → most

Lesson 14 · 99

Lesson 15
She has lived in Canada, Spain and Korea.

Warm-Up *Match the sentences with the pictures.*

a. He **has climbed** Mount Halla.
b. He **has visited** Sydney.
c. He **has lived** abroad.
d. He **has worked** as a volunteer.
e. He **has watched** the Super Bowl.
f. He **has tried** Thai food.
g. He **has traveled** to China.
h. He **has cooked** an Italian dish.
i. He **has surfed** in Hawaii.
j. He **has learned** to scuba dive.

Dialogue *Listen to the dialogue and practice.*

Melinda: Did you hear about Sally?
Brad: What about her?
Melinda: She's a very talented girl.
Brad: Is that so?
Melinda: Yes. She can speak English, Spanish and Korean.
Brad: Wow! How did she learn all those languages?
Melinda: **She has lived in Canada, Spain and Korea.**
Brad: That's awesome!

Comprehension Check!

How many languages can Sally speak?
In which countries has Sally lived?

Role-Play

Using the above dialogue, roleplay with your partner using your own personal information.

Lesson 15 • 101

Grammar Point 1 *Past Participles : Regular Verbs*

Base Verb	Simple Past	Past Participle	Base Verb	Simple Past	Past Participle
climb	climbed	climbed	travel	traveled	traveled
cook	cooked	cooked	try	tried	tried
learn	learned	learned	visit	visited	visited
live	lived	lived	watch	watched	watched
surf	surfed	surfed	work	worked	worked

Grammar Point 2 *Present Perfect: Affirmative & Negative Statements*

Affirmative Statements	Contracted Form
I **have lived** in Canada.	I**'ve lived** in Canada.
You **have visited** Mexico.	You**'ve visited** Mexico.
He / She / It **has surfed** in Hawaii.	He / She / It**'s surfed** in Hawaii.
We **have tried** Chinese food.	We**'ve tried** Chinese food.
You **have watched** the World Cup Final.	You**'ve watched** the World Cup Final.
They **have traveled** all over Europe.	They**'ve traveled** all over Europe.

Negative Statements	
haven't + p.p	**have never + p.p.**
I **haven't lived** in Canada.	I**'ve never lived** in Canada.
You **haven't visited** Mexico.	You**'ve never visited** Mexico.
He / She / It **hasn't surfed** in Hawaii.	He / She / It**'s never surfed** in Hawaii.
We **haven't tried** Chinese food.	We**'ve never tried** Chinese food.
You **haven't watched** the World Cup Final.	You**'ve never watched** the World Cup Final.
They **haven't traveled** all over Europe.	They**'ve never traveled** all over Europe.

Practice
Practice the dialogue with a partner. See the example below.

Stella

travel abroad

Example

A: Did you hear about **Stella**?
B: What about **her**?
A: **She has traveled abroad**.
B: That's awesome! I have never **traveled abroad**.

Paul and Lisa

learn to scuba dive

Example

A: Did you hear about **Paul and Lisa**?
B: What about **them**?
A: **They have learned to scuba dive**.
B: That's awesome! I have never **learned to scuba dive**.

❶ Jane

climb Mount Everest

❷ Charlie

live in Paris

 **3 Tara and Steven** — try Mexican food	 **4 Brian and Patrick** — watch a soccer game
 **5 Robert and Scott** — visit Hong Kong	 **6 Ashley** — work as a volunteer
 **7 Nancy and Jonathan** — cook a French dish	 **8 Mary and Rebecca** — travel to Egypt
 **9 Jennifer** — try skiing	 **10 Alex** — learn to play the drums

STUDENT A

Divide the class into pairs. One student will be **Student A**, and the other will be **Student B**. Referring to the sample dialogue below, form questions and answers using the information provided.

☺ : What are the three most interesting things that you have done in your life?
☺ : I've learned to scuba dive. I've worked abroad. And I've traveled to many countries, such as Thailand, China, Japan and Canada.
☺ : What are the three things that you want to do, but haven't done in your life so far?
☺ : I haven't climbed a mountain. I haven't tried Indian food. And I have never lived in another country.

Verbs

| climb | travel | live | learn | work | play |
| try | visit | cook | surf | watch | study |

1 Write down three things that you have done and three things that you haven't done

I have …
1.
2.
3.

I haven't …
1.
2.
3.

2 Ask **Student B** questions to complete the table below.

He / She has …
1.
2.
3.

He / She hasn't …
1.
2.
3.

Pair Work

 **STUDENT B**

Divide the class into pairs. One student will be **Student A**, and the other will be **Student B**. Referring to the sample dialogue below, form questions and answers using the information provided.

> ☺ :What are the three most interesting things that you have done in your life?
> ☺ :I've learned to scuba dive. I've worked abroad. And I've traveled to many countries, such as Thailand, China, Japan and Canada.
> ☺ :What are the three things that you wnat to do, but haven't done in your life so far?
> ☺ :I haven't climbed a mountain. I haven't tried Indian food. And I have never lived in another country.

Verbs

climb	travel	live	learn	work	play
try	visit	cook	surf	watch	study

1 Write down three things that you have done and three things that you haven't done

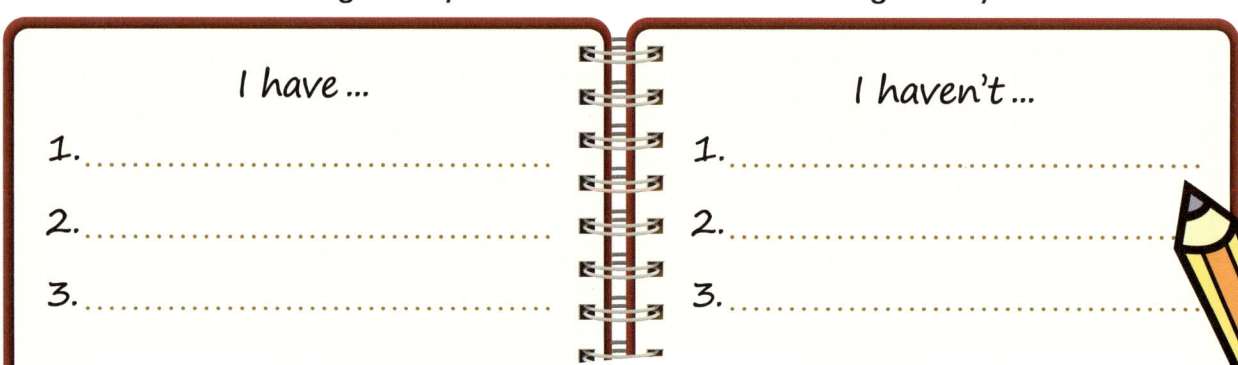

I have ...
1. ....
2. ....
3. ....

I haven't ...
1. ....
2. ....
3. ....

2 Ask **Student A** questions to complete the table below.

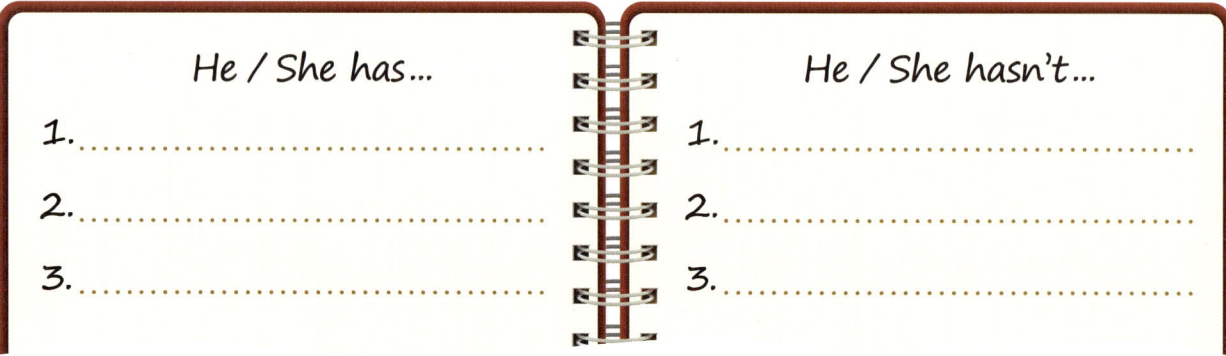

He / She has ...
1. ....
2. ....
3. ....

He / She hasn't ...
1. ....
2. ....
3. ....

Pronunciation
Listen to the following sentences and repeat after them.

1. I have traveled to Australia.
   I've traveled to Australia.

2. He has lived abroad before.
   He hasn't lived abroad before.

3. They haven't tried Mexican food before.
   They've never tried Mexican food before.

4. She hasn't worked as a volunteer.
   He hasn't worked as a volunteer.

5. We have learned to scuba dive.
   We haven't learned to scuba dive.

Stretch Out!

More Regular Past Participles

Base Verb	Simple Past	Past Participle
agree	agreed	agreed
beg	begged	begged
carry	carried	carried
destroy	destoryed	destoryed
found	founded	founded

Base Verb	Simple Past	Past Participle
marry	married	married
play	played	played
reply	replied	replied
stop	stopped	stopped
use	used	used

Lesson 16: Have you ever been to Hong Kong?

Warm-Up *Match the sentences with the pictures.*

a. He **has been** on a diet.
b. She **has had** a pet.
c. He **has ridden** an elephant.
d. He **has won** the lottery.
e. She **has taken** a trip to Brazil.
f. They **have fallen** in love.
g. She **has written** a love letter.
h. He **has met** a celebrity
i. He **has driven** a sports car.
j. They **have flown** in an airplane.
k. She **has gone** skiing.
l. They **have seen** the Eiffel Tower.

Dialogue — Listen to the dialogue and practice.

Adam: Hey, Jenna. Long time no see!
Jenna: Hi, Adam. What a nice surprise! I just came back from my vacation to Hong Kong. *Have you ever been to Hong Kong?*
Adam: *Yes, I have. I've been there once.*
Jenna: *Then, have you seen the Dragon Boat Festival?*
Adam: *No, I haven't seen it.*
Jenna: What a pity! It was an amazing experience. I hope you will see it one day.

Comprehension Check!

Has Jenna been to Hong Kong? | Has Jenna seen the Dragon Boat Festival?
Has Adam been to Hong Kong? | Has Adam seen the Dragon Boat Festival?

Role-Play

Using the above dialogue, roleplay with your partner using your own personal information.

Grammar Point 1 — Past Participle : Irregular Verbs

Base Verb	Simple Past	Past Participle	Base Verb	Simple Past	Past Participle
am / is / are	was / were	been	meet	met	met
drive	drove	driven	ride	rode	ridden
fall	fell	fallen	see	saw	seen
fly	flew	flown	take	took	taken
go	went	gone	win	won	won
have	had	had	write	wrote	written

Lesson 16 · 109

Grammar Point 2 Yes / No Questions and Short Answers

Yes / No Questions	Short Answers	
Have I **(ever) met** you before?	Yes, you **have**.	No, you **haven't**.
Have you **(ever) been** to* Russia?	Yes, I / we **have**.	No, I / we **haven't**.
Has he / she / it **(ever) flown** in an airplane?	Yes, he / she / it **has**.	No, he / she / it **hasn't**.
Have they **(ever) had** a pet?	Yes, they **have**.	No, they **haven't**.

*been (to) = visited

Practice Practice the dialogue with a partner. See the example below.

Sarah and Robert
take a trip to China

Thomas and Becky
take a trip to Japan

Example

A: Have Sarah and Robert ever taken a trip to China?
B: Yes, they have. How about Thomas and Becky?
Have they ever taken a trip to China?
A: No, they haven't, but they've taken a trip to Japan.

1. Joseph — go surfing / Christina — go skiing
2. Vincent — ride a horse / Erica — ride a camel
3. Scott and Terry — be to London / Eric and Mary — be to Paris
4. Angela — have a dog / Steven — have a cat
5. Megan — drive a truck / Jeremy — drive a bus
6. Ana — see the Great Pyramid / Sue — see the London Eye

Divide the class into pairs. One student will be **Student A**, and the other will be **Student B**. Referring to the sample dialogue below, form questions and answers using the information provided.

fly in an airplane

☺ : Have you ever <u>flown in an airplane</u>?
☺ : <u>No</u>, I <u>haven't</u>. Have you?
☺ : <u>Yes</u>, I <u>have</u>. I have <u>flown in an airplane</u>.

win the lottery

☺ : Have you ever <u>won the lottery</u>?
☺ : <u>Yes</u>, I <u>have</u>. Have you?
☺ : <u>No</u>, I <u>haven't</u>. I have never <u>won the lottery</u>.

First, check what you have done in your life so far. Then, ask **Student B** questions about what he / she has done.

Have you …?	You		Your Partner	
	Yes	No	Yes	No
write a love letter	☐	☐	☐	☐
drive a sports car	☐	☐	☐	☐
take a trip to Europe	☐	☐	☐	☐
have a pet	☐	☐	☐	☐
ride an elephant	☐	☐	☐	☐

Pair Work

STUDENT B

Divide the class into pairs. One student will be **Student A**, and the other will be **Student B**. Referring to the sample dialogue below, form questions and answers using the information provided.

fly in an airplane

☺ : Have you ever <u>flown in an airplane</u>?
☺ : <u>No</u>, I <u>haven't</u>. Have you?
☺ : <u>Yes</u>, I <u>have</u>. I have <u>flown in an airplane</u>.

win the lottery

☺ : Have you ever <u>won the lottery</u>?
☺ : <u>Yes</u>, I <u>have</u>. Have you?
☺ : <u>No</u>, I <u>haven't</u>. I have never <u>won the lottery</u>.

First, check what you have done in your life so far. Then, ask **Student A** questions about what he/she has done.

Have you ...?	You		Your Partner	
be on a diet	Yes ☐	No ☐	Yes ☐	No ☐
go skiing	Yes ☐	No ☐	Yes ☐	No ☐
fall in love	Yes ☐	No ☐	Yes ☐	No ☐
see the Eiffel Tower	Yes ☐	No ☐	Yes ☐	No ☐
meet a celebrity	Yes ☐	No ☐	Yes ☐	No ☐

Pronunciation *Listen to the following sentences and repeat after them.*

 1 Have you **been** to Paris?
Have you **seen** the Eiffel Tower?

 2 Has he ever **ridden** an elephant?
Has he ever **written** a love letter?

 3 Have you ever **fallen** in love?
Have you ever **taken** a trip to East Asia?

 4 Has she ever **gone** skiing?
Has she ever **won** the lottery?

 5 Has **she** ever driven a sports car?
Have **they** ever driven a sports car?

Stretch Out!

More Irregular Past Participles

Base Verb	Simple Past	Past Participle
begin	began	begun
come	came	come
drink	drank	drunk
eat	ate	eaten
find	found	found
get	got	gotten

Base Verb	Simple Past	Past Participle
keep	kept	kept
leave	left	left
make	made	made
put	put	put
say	said	said
think	thought	thought

Lesson 17: The convenience store is next to the coffee shop.

Warm-Up *Fill in the blanks with proper prepositions of places.*

– Prepositions –

| on | behind | next to / beside |
| in front of | between | across from |

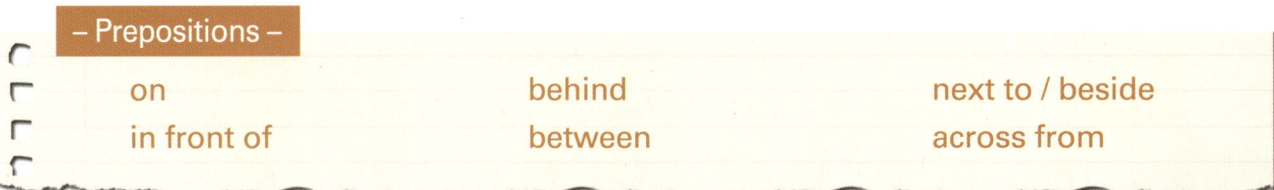

1. The convenience store is _____ the coffee shop.
2. The bakery is _____ the parking lot.
3. The gas station is _____ the convenience store.
4. The DVD rental shop is _____ Fifth Avenue.
5. The fitness center is _____ the drugstore and the beauty salon.
6. The shopping mall is _____ the DVD rental shop.

Dialogue  Listen to the dialogue and practice.

Joshua: Excuse me.
　　　　Is there a convenience store around here?
Ashley: Yeah, there's one near the bus stop.
Joshua: I'm new to the area.
　　　　I don't know where the bus stop is.
Ashley: OK. Do you see the coffee shop on the corner? *The convenience store is next to the coffee shop.*
Joshua: Got it. Thanks a lot.
Ashley: No problem.

Comprehension Check!
Is there a convenience store nearby?
What is next to the convenience store?

Role-Play
Using the above dialogue, roleplay with your partner using your own personal information.

Grammar Point 1 — Describing Locations

Questions	Answers
Is there a drugstore around here?	Yes, there's one **on** Fourth Avenue.
	No, there aren't any around here.
Where is the shopping mall?	It's **across from** the fitness center.
	It's **between** the bank **and** the hotel.

Lesson 17 · 115

Grammar Point 2 *Prepositions of Places*

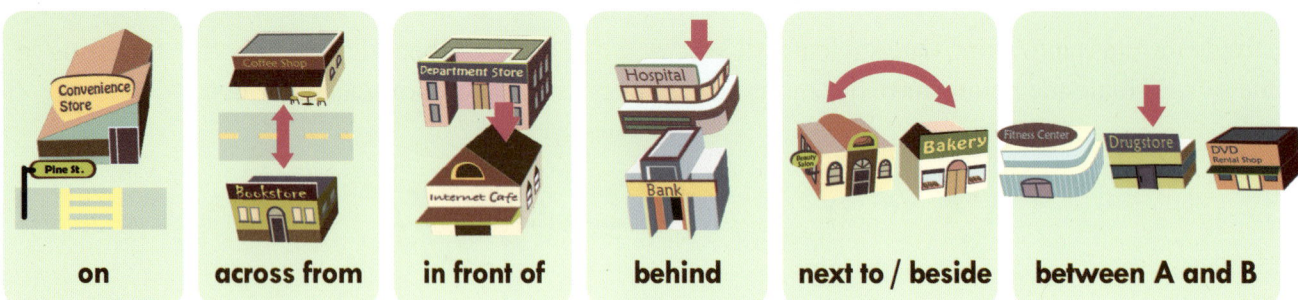

| on | across from | in front of | behind | next to / beside | between A and B |

Practice *Practice the dialogue with a partner. See the example below.*

Example

A: Excuse me. May I ask you something?
B: Sure, what is it?
A: Is there a <u>drugstore</u> around here?
B: Yes, the drugstore is <u>in front of the hospital</u>.

STUDENT A

Divide the class into pairs. One student will be **Student A**, and the other will be **Student B**. Referring to the sample dialogue below, form questions and answers using the information provided.

😀 : Is the coffee shop located on Fifth Avenue?
🙂 : Yes, it is.
😀 : Is the coffee shop located next to the bus stop?
🙂 : No, it isn't.
😀 : Is the coffee shop located in front of the bank?
🙂 : Yes, it is.

Ask **Student B** questions to find the places below.

❶ Beauty Salon　　❷ DVD Rental Shop　　❸ Gas Station

Lesson 17 • 117

Pair Work

STUDENT B

Divide the class into pairs. One student will be **Student A**, and the other will be **Student B**. Referring to the sample dialogue below, form questions and answers using the information provided.

☺ : Is the coffee shop located on Fifth Avenue?
☺ : Yes, it is.
☺ : Is the coffee shop located next to the bus stop?
☺ : No, it isn't.
☺ : Is the coffee shop located in front of the bank?
☺ : Yes, it is.

Ask **Student A** questions to find the places below.

① Convenience Store   ② Fitness Center   ③ Bakery

Pronunciation Listen to the following sentences and repeat after them.

1. Is there a drugstore around here?
   Is there a convenience store around here?

2. The beauty salon is behind the fitness center.
   The beauty salon is beside the fitness center.

3. It's across from the coffee shop.
   It's across from the DVD rental shop.

4. There's a shopping mall on Fifth Avenue.
   There's a shopping mall on Fifteenth Avenue.

5. Where is the gas station?
   Where is the police station?

Stretch Out!

More Expressions for Describing Location

- The gas station is across from the department store.
  = The gas station is opposite the department store.
  = The gas station is facing the department store.
- The internet cafe is at the end of the block.
- The shoe store is next door to the furniture store.
- The movie theater is on the corner of Fifth Avenue and Walnut Street.

Lesson 17 · 119

Lesson 18
Could you tell me how to get to the library?

Warm-Up Fill in the blanks with proper names of campus buildings.

★ You are here!

1. Go straight for two blocks and turn left. The *student center* is on your right.
2. Turn left at the first corner. The *gymnasium* is on your right.
3. Walk straight for two blocks and turn right. The *snack bar* is on the left.
4. Go straight for one block and make a right turn. The *cafeteria* is on the right.
5. Walk straight for two blocks and turn left. Cross the street and the *dormitory* is on your right.

Dialogue Listen to the dialogue and practice.

Jennie: Excuse me. I'm a freshman. *Could you tell me how to get to the library?*
Andrew: Sure. *Go straight and turn left at the corner.* It's between the student center and the cafeteria.
Jennie: Thanks a lot.
Andrew: You can get a campus map at the student center. You can pick it up on your way to the library.
Jennie: Oh, that sounds good! Thanks a lot.
Andrew: No problem.

Comprehension Check!
Should Jennie turn left or right at the corner? | Is the library located behind the student center?

Role-Play
Using the above dialogue, roleplay with your partner using your own personal information.

Grammar Point 1 *Giving Directions*

Questions	Answers
How can I get to the health center? Could you tell me how to get to the health center?	**Walk straight** for three blocks. (= **Go straight**) **Turn right** at the corner. (= **Make a right turn**) **Turn left** at the corner. (= **Make a left turn**) **Cross** the street. It's on your right / left.

Lesson 18 • 121

Grammar Point 2 *Imperatives*

Affirmative Statements	Negative Statements
Go straight.	**Don't go** straight.
Turn right.	**Don't turn** right.
Make a left turn.	**Don't make** a left turn.
Cross the street.	**Don't cross** the street.

Practice Practice the dialogue with a partner. See the example below.

> Example
>
> A: How do I get to the <u>bookstore</u> from here?
> B: Go straight and <u>make a left turn</u> at the corner.
>   It's on your <u>right</u> next to the <u>tennis court</u>.
> A: Thanks a lot.
> B: No problem.

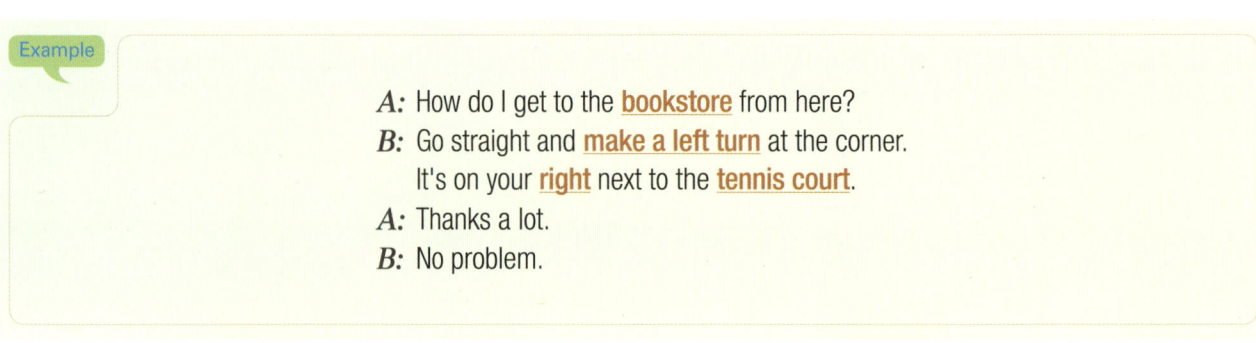

★ You are here!

STUDENT A

Divide the class into pairs. One student will be **Student A**, and the other will be **Student B**. Referring to the sample dialogue below, find out the locations of the places on the map.

☺ : Excuse me, can you tell me how to get to the <u>parking area</u>?
☺ : Sure. <u>Go straight for two blocks and turn left</u>. <u>The parking area is on your right</u>.

Ask **Student B** for directions to find the places below.

| Student Center | Main Library | Health Center |

Parking Area | Gymnasium
Snack Bar
Basketball Court | Cafeteria
Bookstore | Domitory

★ You are here!

Lesson 18 · 123

Pair Work

 **STUDENT B**

Divide the class into pairs. One student will be **Student A**, and the other will be **Student B**. Referring to the sample dialogue below, find out the locations of the places on the map.

☺ : Excuse me, can you tell me how to get to the **parking area**?
☺ : Sure. **Go straight for two blocks and turn left**.
    The parking area is on your right.

Ask **Student A** for directions to find the places below.

| Cafeteria | Gymnasium | Snack Bar |

Pronunciation *Listen to the following sentences and repeat after them.*

1. How can I get to the health center?
   How can I get to the student center?

2. Go straight for two blocks.
   Walk straight for two blocks.

3. Make a right turn at the second corner.
   Make a left turn at the second corner.

4. Turn left and cross the street.
   Turn left but don't cross the street.

5. Could you tell me how to get to the dormitory?
   Could you tell me how to get to the gymnasium?

Stretch Out!

More Words for Giving Directions

intersection	traffic light	corner	crosswalk

stop sign	road sign	overpass	tunnel

NOTE

NOTE

NOTE